Palace Gate

Richard L. Brown

Under Siege in Hue City
TET
January 1968

PALACE GATE

Lt.Col. Richard L. Brown
(USAF, Ret.)

Schiffer Military/Aviation History
Atglen, PA

Dedication
To Janice. She has made life a pleasure.

In Appreciation

Fellow FAC Robert C. Mikesh, who provided essential help in manuscript preparation and marketing plus many photographs.

Friend and spouse for 47 years, Janice, who worked the word processor, spell-checker and all the other details that turn scribbled thoughts into a book.

Book Design by Robert Biondi.

Library of Congress Catalog Number: 95-67279

Printed in the United States of America.
ISBN: 0-88740-745-4

We are interested in hearing from authors with book ideas on related topics.

Published by Schiffer Publishing Ltd.
77 Lower Valley Road
Atglen, PA 19310
Please write for a free catalog.
This book may be purchased from the publisher.
Please include $2.95 postage.
Try your bookstore first.

CONTENTS

FOREWORD

This is a book about life as seen by the eyes of a typical (non-hero) military pilot. My Vietnam experience didn't produce a lot of hang-ups. I hated the "scum-bag" label a few people gave me, and I drank a little too much for a month or two. Once I accepted the fact that most people just didn't want to know anything about what was happening over there, everything returned to normal. Now I am pleased by the increasing interest in Vietnam and public acceptance of the great tragedy it was.

People who haven't experienced all-out war will never realize just how violent it is. The sounds alone are enough to put some people into shock.

Perhaps, I thought, our friends at home could get a better idea of what it was like if I recorded a mortar attack on the Military Advisory Corps, Vietnam (MACV) Compound in Hue, where I lived. It happened that the first attack where I remembered to start the tape recorder turned into a real battle, the 1968 Tet offensive. During the first four days of the battle I took a few moments to make correspondence tapes for my family, describing the battle, problems and, incidentally, a lot of combat sounds. Capture of the MACV compound was a major goal of the invading NVA forces and the situation (surrounded and out-numbered) was a little like the Alamo except reinforcements (U.S. Marines) did arrive.

Minutes before I left the MACV compound to join General Truong on the other side of Hue, I handed the boxed tapes to one of my pilots and asked him to mail them to my wife if and when he got to Da Nang. I thought the tapes would at least prove I was alive and well as of that date.

As luck would have it, they all arrived at home the same day and, as luck would have it, the first one she played was the one made when the battle started. I wasn't in the room and there were no comments – just the sounds of rockets, mortars, machine guns and grenades at close range. She didn't think it was funny. I was returned to good graces when she flipped the reel over and my voice was there to assure her I was relatively secure.

An audio cassette containing fifty minutes of these "real time" comments and sounds of the battle around the MACV compound is available. Call 1-512-884-4751 for more information. I recommend reading to the end of chapter seven before playing the tape. (Schiffer Publishing Ltd. is not associated with this offer).

Many of the names of people mentioned in this book have been changed to protect individuals' privacy. Conversations, where I have used quotations, may not contain the exact words uttered but do reflect, to the best of my ability, the meaning and context of those communications. Quotes from my tapes and letters are exactly as recorded and/or written.

Glossary

Actual	Word used in radio transmissions to distinguish between the radio operator and the person the call sign is actually assigned to.
AK-47	Russian or Chinese-made automatic rifle which fired a small, high-velocity bullet.
ALO	Air Liaison Officer
ARVN	Army of the Republic of Vietnam
BDA	Bomb Damage Assessment
B-40	A Chinese anti-tank rocket, shoulder fired. It used a shaped charge and could punch through seven inches of steel.
Bingo	Time at which there is only sufficient fuel to return to base with minimum reserve.
CBU	Cluster Bomb Unit, composed of a large number of small bombs, somewhat larger than hand grenades, with air drag fins for slow descent; primarily anti-personnel weapon.
CONEX	Large steel boxes, about 6 feet by 10 feet square, designed as shipping compartments but commonly used for storage since they could be locked and were very sturdy.
CP	Command Post
DASC	Direct Air Support Center, central dispatch for all missions involved in direct air support.
DMZ	De-Militarized Zone
FAC	A pilot who, from a forward ground or airborne position, controls aircraft involved in close air support of troops.
Free Fire Zone	A designated area where anyone or anything can be killed or destroyed.
HE	A high explosive rocket or artillery shell.
H and I	Harassment and Interdiction; shells fired at intervals to harass or interrupt enemy actions.

IP	Initial Point, usually for the beginning of a bomb run.
LZ	Landing Zone
MACV	Military Assistance Command Vietnam
M-16	Standard rifle, automatic firing, carried by most American troops.
M-79	A shotgun-like device that propelled a small explosive charge, similar to a hand grenade, a distance several times farther than could be thrown.
NVA	North Vietnamese Army
Pemmican	Dried meat pounded into a powder and mixed with hot fat and dried fruits or berries, pressed into a loaf or small cakes.
RF	Regional Forces, Vietnamese military forces usually controlled by Province Chiefs.
R & R	Rest and Relaxation leave
SAC	Strategic Air Command
Spooky	A C-47 with Vulcan, very high output, guns set up to shoot out the side of the plane. Fire could be concentrated in a small area by flying in a tight circle that kept the guns aimed at a point and the bullet-stream describing a cone.
Slick	A helicopter with no guns, used to carry personnel or supplies.
TOC	Tactical Operations Center
Tracer	Bullet with a phosphorous insert that burns brilliantly to trace its trajectory.
VC	Viet Cong
WP	A rocket or shell containing white phosphorus that makes a dense white cloud when detonated.

Chapter 1

A Government-Sponsored Adventureland

A twelve -year old boy, lying on the floor, was looking at a book so big and heavy he couldn't hold it on his lap. It was a history of World War I with lots of photographs, maps and detailed accounts of United States involvement. He looked up at his mother and said, "I hope there won't be another war until I'm old enough to get in it." She reminded him of his comment many times during the next 32 years.

Mother was 85 when I came back from Vietnam in 1968, my third war. I was surprised to learn that she had been worried about me. The details of our conversation have faded but the thrust remains clear – "Have you had enough?"

"Yes, not so much because of the hazards, but my uncertainties regarding cost versus gain."

China (where I flew during World War II) had been lost to Communism, a stalemate remained in Korea and, where I had been in Vietnam, we were steadily losing a war that held little promise of gain for the individuals involved regardless of which side won.

I was in college on Pearl Harbor Day, December 7, 1941 and remained there working on a degree in aeronautical engineering until the lure of flying and adventure became too strong. In the fall of 1942 I joined the Army Air Corps Aviation Cadet program.

Active duty began in February, 1943, starting with the series of training phases that were finalized in the spring of 1944 by awarding me some wings and a pair of second lieutenant's bars to pin on my uniform. Along with the hardware for my uniform were orders to begin fighter pilot training. That included gunnery practice in T-6s at Matagorda Island in the Gulf of Mexico, to be followed by ten hours of orientation flying in P-40s at Foster Field, Texas.

Fighter pilot training was a disappointment since I'd checked twin-engine bombers in several questionnaires administered to aviation cadets and the B-26 was my airplane of choice. I loved low altitude flying and had spent many risky hours buzzing imaginary targets but it was wartime and you took what they gave you. Fighters it would be.

We returned to Foster Field from T-6 gunnery training at Matagorda Island on a Friday. That afternoon we were given some cockpit time in P-40s for familiarization. The planes we had to fly were an assortment of odd models and series – no two alike. I remember seeing P-40Es, Js, and Ns. They were unsophisticated airplanes. Flap and landing gear controls were simply hydraulic valves bolted to the side of the cockpit with bent pieces of metal that served as handles. A long axe handle-like affair along the right side of the seat controlled the radiator doors. There was no engine coolant thermostat; the pilot watched the temperature gauge and adjusted the doors to keep the engine temperature within limits. I could see that the step from T-6s to P-40s was going to be a big one. There were no dual cockpit trainers or flight simulators – you just got in and flew it.

Transition flying was to begin Saturday but low clouds and rain kept us sitting around in the flight line shack until late in the afternoon when a captain announced there would be no flying until Monday morning. We had just spent two weeks on Matagorda Island with no girls and little entertainment other than fishing. We headed for town, Victoria, at top speed.

Dale Morgan and I decided to get a bottle of whiskey and go to a Texas style B.Y.O.B. club that had good steaks, music and, usually, a few spare girls. American whiskey was sometimes hard to find during the war years. That night, it proved impossible. We settled for a fifth of something called Mexican cane whiskey, 100 proof. The steaks were good, we managed to get a few dances but at the end of the evening, all we had was one empty bottle and two inebriated brains.

We headed for the telephone to call a cab. Walking created a strange floating sensation with a vague awareness of chairs and tables getting in the way – falling over. Somehow we got back to our iron cots in open barracks. My bed started doing slow rolls as soon as I lay down. It was a new experience and so vivid I held on to the frame tightly to keep from falling out when the bed was upside down. After doing what seemed like 100 rolls, my stomach began to complain. I thought I was going to be air sick if I didn't stop the slow rolls. I opened my eyes and made the bed stop spinning. It was a tough fight but I managed to go to sleep before throwing up.

What seemed like a few seconds later, someone was shaking me. It was a sergeant, going from bed to bed, waking up everyone in the room. My head was throbbing, my stomach queasy, every nerve in my body was complaining about the cane whiskey treatment. I looked at my watch – six o'clock in the morning! What the hell was going on?

When a significant percentage of us were at least sitting up, the sergeant announced, "Everybody down to the flight shack immediately. Flying will start at Oh-700." We complained, said we were told no flying until Monday. The sergeant said, "That was the plan yesterday; today the plan is to fly today and that's that."

I hadn't made the transition from almost blind obedience expected of cadets to an officer capable of thinking. If I told them I wasn't sober, what would happen? My only hope was that I wouldn't be scheduled for 7:00 and I'd have a few more hours to recover. I didn't want to make my first P-40 flight until I felt a lot better than I did then.

Moving slowly to avoid a reoccurrence of the slow rolls, I pulled on a flight suit and walked down to the flight shack. I didn't eat or drink anything – my stomach wouldn't take it.

Inside, I checked the flight schedule on the blackboard. There it was – Brown, Richard L.: take-off time: 0700. Curses!

Alphabetical order syndrome common to all Army scheduling had done me again. I stood there contemplating possible choices – go in the latrine and throw up (messy), go on sick call (too late for that), slip out the door and claim I had shacked up with a girl and not returned until afternoon (too many had seen me). Before I could decide, an instructor walked into the room and called out six names, including mine. We sat down at a picnic style table with the instructor standing at one end. He passed out mimeographed sheets describing what we were to do during our first flight, such as climb to altitude, practice gear and flap extensions, slow flying and coordination practice such as lazy eights, chandelles, etc.

His briefing lasted all of three minutes then it was time to check out a parachute and find your airplane. Mine was the first one in the line. Damn it!! Everything was happening too fast.

A crew chief leaned in the cockpit and showed me how to start the engine. Good God! It was a big noisy thing. My head was throbbing like the engine, my mouth was dry as parchment, I hurt so bad that death did not seem an unpleasant alternative.

The engine was running smoothly; the crew chief and his assistant were standing ready to pull the chocks. There was nothing I could do but signal with my thumbs to pull them out of the way and start my taxi – the sooner I took off the sooner I could land.

My next memory of the flight was climbing to 10,000 feet, where it was cooler and just circling for about a half hour. I had difficulty reading the instruction sheet; every time I put my head down I got dizzy. After one attempt I looked up just in time to see another P-40 cross just 100 feet or so in front of me. He was probably looking at his instruction sheet too.

Time was running out. I had to go back down and land the beast so, abandoning the prescribed routine, I just dumped the gear and flaps and practiced approaches and slow flight while descending.

They had positioned an instructor in a mobile control 'tower' on the back of a truck near the end of the runway. His job was to coach us during our first approach and landing with phrases such as 'put your gear down', 'you forgot your flaps', 'you're too high', 'too low', 'too fast', 'too slow', 'go around and try again', etc. I turned towards the base and switched to the mobile tower frequency.

It was total chaos. Some guys were on their third or fourth tries to land. The instructor was screaming invectives, making everyone tighten up and over-control. Several planes, damaged by ground loops, blown tires and broken tail wheels, were waiting in the grass along the runway for tugs and maintenance crews. I was hurting so bad it didn't matter – they could have had anti-aircraft guns out there, trying to shoot us down. My goal then was two aspirin and a coke (current cure for a hangover).

Waves of nausea hit while I was in the long base leg landing pattern and my primary objective shifted to not throwing up – what the plane was doing mattered much less. At last I was on final approach. The instructor was mercifully quiet. Over the end of the runway, I cut the throttle, flared to an approximate landing attitude and waited for the crash or whatever. I really didn't care. I waited some more then felt a rhythmic vibration – what was it? As time wore on and the plane continued to slow down, I decided it had to be the tar strips on the runway – I had landed. Either I was so numb I couldn't feel the wheels hit the runway or the landing was so smooth there was no tell-tale bump.

Bile was rising in my throat as I walked back to the flight shack. I threw up seconds after getting into the latrine. A little later all flying was canceled – there were hardly any P-40s still in flying condition.

When all planes were back on the ground, it was time for a critique. The mobile tower officer came in with a clipboard in hand and a scowl on his face that would stop a clock. After a ten-minute tirade on our collective ineptitude, he started on the details. Each pilot had to stand when his name was called, then bear the shame of having his approach and landing mistakes described in detail in public. I stood, not really caring, just thankful to have survived. He looked at his clipboard, then at me, and said, "Good landing." How I could feel so good and hurt so bad at the same time?

Thankfully, the mobile control tower was not out on the runway for any of my following P-40 landings. They weren't nearly as good.

Bruning Army Air Field in south central Nebraska was my next assignment. There I received P-47 transition and combat training. Our graduation class was smaller than most. Of the sixty students who stepped off the buses on a sunny afternoon to begin their P-47 training, only twenty-eight got back on the buses two months later. Twenty-eight had been killed, two were in the hospital and two had been washed out.

As we were standing along side the buses waiting for room assignments, an odd sound from above directed our attention to the blue sky. A P-47 and a B-17 had collided almost directly over the field. The B-17 fluttered down with a few parachutes blossoming along the way. The P-47 went into a straight down dive – no chute. Twin columns of black smoke were high in the sky southeast of the base as we picked up our bags and headed for the BOQs (Bachelor Officers' Quarters). They consisted of one-story tar-paper covered shacks divided by low partitions into ten cubbyholes, each furnished with two iron frame cots.

The class was divided into three twenty-man groups for ease of scheduling the various training phases. For some reason, room assignments were in alphabetical order but the first two training groups were set up with every other name in alphabetical order, the balance in the third. There were four Browns in the class, three with the same first initial, R, and one of them had the same first name as mine.

It seemed our class fortune was destined to continue in step with the mid-air collision we witnessed as we arrived. Within days, things started to happen.

My oxygen mask was giving me problems so one morning I headed for the personal equipment section to get it repaired. The repair shop was in the northern-most building of the supply area, near the end of the northwest/southeast runway. I was standing on a corner, waiting for the base bus, killing time watching the guys practice landings. It was a good spot because they were landing to the southeast. I had an unobstructed view of their approaches, turns onto final and landings. The P-47 was a heavy plane with lots of drag in landing configuration. It didn't glide. Without power, it dropped like a brick.

One of the planes on the base leg was going slower than most, nose high. I became concerned when it was obvious he was late starting his turn toward the runway. Like someone might do when he could see his plane was going beyond the end of the runway, he kicked in extra bottom rudder to speed the turn. The low wing stalled and the plane snap-rolled to the left. He remembered his basic lessons, stuck the nose down and added power. It wasn't enough; he was too low. He tried to pull the nose up and stalled again. This time it snapped to the right and he hit – hard. The P-47 disintegrated with a terrible crunch and a fire ball. I didn't see how anyone could have survived but I ran towards it, hoping. The engine had rolled about 100 feet ahead of the fire. Between it and flames there was a motionless object. The size and color was about right. It could be the pilot. It was!

He was still strapped in his seat, lying on one side with his face pressed down in the dirt. As I got closer I could see his cloth helmet had been torn off. It had to be Charlie Fox. I'd recognize his reddish-brown crew cut hair anywhere. We were class-mates all the way through Cadets. There was a hole the size of a quarter in the back of his head. Not good but possibly not fatal. I started to roll him over so he could breath but then I saw it wasn't necessary – the front half of his head was gone.

Accidents kept on happening. I guess it wasn't unexpected. One of the characteristics given strong consideration when selecting people for fighter training was aggressive personalities, especially when flying. We were not low-risk people. Take a group of aggressive, inexperienced (about 250 flying hours) pilots and stick them in 2,200 horsepower single engine airplanes built for aggressive flying and things will happen. Eight of our class died in P-47 training crashes.

During the second month of training the three groups were each scheduled for ten days of gunnery and dive bomb training near Pierre, South Dakota. The first group left for Pierre in a C-47 on a day when thunderheads were building up. The plane was seen in northern Nebraska, falling out of a storm cloud in pieces. All twenty-eight on board were killed, including twenty classmates, two of whom were Browns, including the other Richard. The next day my group was flown up to replace them.

I had been in Pierre about a week when a Western Union operator located me. It was a telegram from my sister and the message was so unusual I remember every word. "Letter returned marked deceased. Why didn't you tell me?"

It seems the mail clerks at Bruning had been a little confused about which Browns had been killed. Since I wasn't there to collect my mail, it was stamped "deceased" and returned. I called my sister and asked her to explain the rationale that led to the curious wording in her telegram. She simply didn't accept the idea that I'd been killed and was mad because I hadn't let her know there had been an incident where someone might have been concerned about my fate. I thought it was funny; she didn't.

It so happened that our BOQ caught most of the losses. One night there were just two of us in the place. Since survivors totaled only four or five, we moved to one end for company.

The Officers' Open Mess wasn't doing well financially. Looking around for ways to save money, the mess officer noticed that cube sugar, not the fine grain, wrapped in paper kind, but the naked, rock hard, non-granulated sugar, was cheap. He directed that all sugar would be purchased in cube form. The cooks had to use the cubes, too. Lumpy desserts were the norm. Cubes added to iced tea would still have square corners fifteen minutes later unless violent crushing actions were taken with knife handles or king-sized G.I. spoons. They even resisted dissolving in hot coffee. The ultimate irritation was trying to put sugar on cold breakfast cereal such as corn flakes. The best technique was to place a cube in the palm of one hand and hit it with the back of a spoon. It helped to imagine the face of the mess officer on each cube. The mess hall sounded like a carpenter's shop every morning as pilots tried to crush the rocklike cubes.

The nearest town where anyone could have fun (spelled bars and girls) was Beatrice – about 40 miles on a gravel road, due east. Four of us bought a 1934 Plymouth from a graduating pilot so we could get into town on weekends. It was a wreck but it ran. The big problem was brakes. The brake pedal did nothing whatever about slowing the car; however, the parking brake still worked to a limited extent. The car could be driven so long as the driver used judicious planning on all stops. There was no allowance for emergency stops – only evasive actions.

After four or five trips to town, the emergency brake failed completely but, by then, we had developed techniques such as shutting the engine off while in low gear, down to opening the doors and dragging our feet when it appeared velocity was still too high as we approached the desired stopping point. Some of the things I remember about trips to town in the Plymouth were:

– The night someone challenged Dave to drive all the way to Beatrice on the left side of the road. He did it without a scratch by slowing down and waving wildly for oncoming cars (there weren't many) to move over to the other side.

– An impulsive turn into a corner gas station at too high a speed, hurtling through it, then out around the intersection in a large circle while down-shifting and dragging feet to get it stopped on the next pass – the attendant just standing there, smiling.

– Pulling into a diagonal parking spot in downtown Beatrice on a busy Saturday night with too much speed, bouncing over the curb onto the busy sidewalk while people dodged or just sat there on benches and watched.

– Opening my eyes at 2:00 A.M. to see nothing but six-foot high weeds in the headlights, being flailed by the bumper as we crashed through them. I was in the right front seat. I looked at the driver; he was just waking up too. He said, "Where the hell is the road?" I guessed to the left and pointed that way. He turned the wheel and the car tipped on two wheels as it climbed a steep bank then crashed down on all four when landing on the road. The two passengers in the back never knew what happened. On the next trip to town, we showed them the quarter-mile swath our car had made down in the bottom of the ditch.

The car was in such bad shape we didn't try to sell it. The driver's seat had broken down to the point where it had to be propped up on two whiskey bottles; the tires were bad and, of course, absolutely no brakes. We left it in the club parking lot with the keys in the ignition. It still ran.

Class losses didn't put much of a damper on our flying and recreational activities. One time a classmate and I were positioned on the green carpet in front of the base commander's desk and accused of flying under a bridge in St. Joseph, Missouri. It was true that my wing man, Dave Brace, had landed with a three-foot section of heavy steel cable in the leading edge of his wing and scratches all over the propeller and engine cowling where he'd hit the cable head on. However, we really hadn't flown under a bridge; the cable had been maybe one hundred feet above the river, between the bridges. I had been the leader of a two-ship low altitude cross country training flight. We were very low when flying up the river at St. Joseph but we definitely went *over* the bridges.

About the time we were busy denying any flying below two hundred feet (the prescribed minimum), the C.O.'s phone rang. It was, we were told, an official from St. Joseph and he was complaining that two P-47s had created a disturbance over their town including such acts as flying under a bridge. The C.O. told the caller he had the pilots in question standing in front of him and he could rest assured they would be punished. The damaged plane was a brand new D-30 model with a bubble canopy, the first on base and the C.O.'s pet airplane. We expected some punishment but not this accusation. Dave and I looked at each other in amazement – it simply wasn't true. We maintained our innocence despite the C.O.'s red face, shouting and pounding on his desk. Finally, we were dismissed from the kangaroo court with a promise that we would regret our actions.

We kept waiting for the ax to fall but it didn't. Dave and I were sitting together at the bar in the officers' club the night before we left for overseas assignments. The base adjutant, who had had a few drinks, staggered up between our stools, draped his arms around our shoulders and said he felt like a shit about what he had done but the C.O. made him do it. It turned out the phone call had been faked – it came from his desk in the next room!

Powerful airplanes, violent flying, girls, booze and adventure. Many of us were under 21 but no one ever questioned our right to buy liquor. It was a wild, wonderful time. I enjoyed it to the hilt. War was all I had hoped it would be and I hadn't even gotten to combat yet.

As it turned out, training was more exciting for me than combat. The Japanese in China were largely on the defensive by the time I got there. The unit I was assigned to (91st Fighter Squadron, 81st Fighter Group) was based at Sian, the northern most 14th Air Force air field in China. The closest Japanese troops ran a radar station at the Yellow River Bend, about 40 miles east of us. Sian had the longest supply line (Calcutta, India was the nearest friendly port) and P-47s used lots of gas so it was a long time between missions. The little combat experience I received was confined to bombing railroads and strafing trains. Boredom was our biggest problem. Operational losses (planes and people lost to weather, malfunctions or pilot error) were greater than combat losses.

Fuel was so precious we rarely taxied the P-47s; instead they were towed to the end of the gravel runway by alcohol-burning jeeps. We took off as soon as the engine was running smoothly using sixty-five inches (mercury) manifold pressure and water injection. The combination of a full combat-load of bombs, ammo, drop tank and a short, dusty runway was hard on engines. When landing, we cut the fuel off (idle cut-off) as soon as the wheels were on the ground, rolled off the runway to either side and waited for a tow back to the revetment.

The one hangar at Sian had marks to show that the Japanese had been active in the area at one time. Its curved metal roof resembled a huge upside-down colander with probably a thousand bullet holes in it.

Just a few days after the war ended, a group of seven or eight pilots ferried P-47s down to Chengtu for some now forgotten reason. I was one of them. As usual, transportation arrangements were loose, informal and largely left up to personal initiative. We sat around Chengtu for two days waiting for promised rides back to Sian but nothing materialized. Things were chaotic. Someone in base operations mentioned that a C-47 parked near the north end of the ramp was currently not assigned to any organization. The former 'owners', a small, clandestine group (probably OSI) had pulled out, just leaving the plane sitting there. If we took it, who cared? The Chinese Nationalists were going to get everything anyway.

None of us were C-47 pilots. In fact, only Carl Overstreet (we called him Subway) had ever flown an airplane with two engines –he had some P-38 flying time.

We walked north. The plane looked bad, covered with dust, the interior had been stripped, no cargo compartment seats, only one seat-belt in the whole airplane. Thank God, it was on the pilot's seat. All the radios except for one VHF set had been pulled out.

Subway said he'd check it out, see if he could figure out how to start the engines and test the radio. Fortunately, the C-47 had all kinds of instructional placards and labels on the various controls, such as landing gear, flaps, tail-wheel lock, etc. Engine and flight controls pretty much worked the same on all planes in those days.

He flicked the battery switch on. A host of needles on the panel jumped to their proper positions. We had juice! Things started humming. Within a few minutes both engines were running and the tower reported that our radio was weak but clear. Magnetos checked okay and all tanks were full so he shut the engines off and we headed back to get our bags.

While filing a clearance at Operations, several people waiting for rides to Sian asked if they could go too. "Sure. Why not?" No one bothered to tell them the exact situation with regard to flight crew or aircraft qualifications.

We climbed in, threw our ungainly seat-pack parachutes and bags in the back end and, except for Subway and Eli, who had been elected to fly co-pilot, sat on the floor and pulled out the cards.

The area between Chengtu and Sian is mostly mountainous with ridges about 9,000 to 10,000 feet high. It was a weather factory. Sian and Chengtu weather was okay but no one knew what the weather was between the two cities. The weatherman made the usual guesses but no one knew.

We had been in the air and climbing for about thirty minutes when a strong smoke odor hit our nostrils. After a few minutes of fruitless sniffing around the cockpit, someone opened a door in the back end that provided access to the tail cone area. Smoke rolled out. There was a big radio chassis back there (our only radio) and it was in flames.

People started running around frantically looking for a fire extinguisher. There wasn't any. The only thing anyone came up with was a crash ax – a gadget usually strapped to the bulkhead at the front of the cabin and intended for use by occupants in the event the plane crashed and they were trapped inside.

A couple of guys chopped the burning radio out of its rubber mounts while we got the bail-out hatch open – no small task. Using the pointed hook end of the ax, they dragged it out of the compartment and kicked it out the door.

We closed the hatch and went back to playing poker. By now we were flying in clouds. A solid cloud layer covered the mountain ridges so we had to fly on instruments. It was no sweat. We'd fly on a thirty degree heading for about two more hours (Sian weather was okay the last we heard) then start looking for a hole. It was drier on the north side of the mountains and weather was usually better.

Maybe another half hour passed and the game was going good when all of us, the money and cards rose off the floor about one foot then crashed down hard. Several offered some verbal guidance to the pilots such as "Don't you know how to fly instruments?" and a few profane comments were made as we attempted to get the cards and money back into correct positions.

Before that was accomplished there was a solid whomp on the bottom of the plane and we began a multi-'G' pull-up. People were forced into weird positions by virtue of their previous crosslegged or spread-legged positions on the floor. Now we were really unhappy about our chauffeurs. What the hell was going on up there in front?

Before any serious complaints could be voiced, there was an instant reversal of forces. Wham! In a split second we were plastered as hard against the ceiling as we had been on the floor. It was a tangled mass of humanity. I happened to be in a position I could see into Eli's side of the cockpit. His head and shoulders were up against the roof too – still holding onto the wheel (lower ceiling).

Two or three more violent trips to the floor and ceiling convinced us that something was terribly wrong. Wind noise was awesome. Someone yelled back from the cockpit to 'get out.' The word passed instantly but the chutes and bail-out hatch were in back. First on the ceiling and then on the floor, again on the ceiling and again on the floor the tangled mass of pilots and hapless passengers struggled towards the rear. Some of the passengers didn't have chutes but, I have to confess, that didn't enter my mind at the time.

Things inside the cabin began to look bad. Someone had 'liberated' an officers' mess kit (a box containing table settings of china and silver for about twenty people) in Chengtu. It had broken open and knives, forks, spoons and dishes were flying all over the cabin. Faces and hands were bloody.

I made it back where the chutes were but couldn't find mine. Each had the pilot's name stenciled on the straps and had been carefully fitted. I assumed, like others, that chutes were up for grabs. I started pulling one on but it was so small I couldn't get the straps over my shoulders. No good. During another trip to the ceiling my face landed on Charlie Bennett's chest. There was my name right in front of my eyes. I pushed back, indicating I wanted my chute. Charlie was the smallest pilot in the outfit. He looked at me and pointed to the strap where the names were painted. I looked. It was his. I think that chute exchange was one of the quickest ever made.

Some of the guys had already found suitable chutes and were working on opening the hatch. Terrific wind pressure (Subway told us later the airspeed indicator had pegged at 300 mph) was making it very hard to pull the hatch open. I waited, hanging on to the bare aluminum interior structure of the plane, next to the bailout station, just ahead of the hatch.

I had time to think about leaving the plane. We were in the center of the mountains. It would be a long barefoot walk back because I was (against regulations) wearing low-cut shoes. They would come off the second the chute opened. I decided I didn't want to leave the plane unless absolutely necessary but would be the first one to the door.

The men pulling on the hatch fell back across the cabin as the door finally popped loose. I stepped towards the opening. Just as I got into the doorway, the color outside turned from gray to green. We were in a steep dive, coming out the bottom of a cloud. I thought, "I'm going to look ahead; if we are going to hit something I'll just step out and pull the ripcord. If not, I won't go." Despite the furious slipstream, I moved my head outside the door far enough to look ahead along the side of the fuselage. Subway was pulling out of the dive. We were screaming down the middle of a narrow valley. The ridges up ahead went into the clouds on both sides. We had lucked out. There was no need to walk back.

I started to pull back into the plane. I had a good grip on the door frame but couldn't move. Instead, I was being pushed farther out the door by the people behind me – they didn't know what I knew.

I tried to yell back over my shoulder that it was okay but they couldn't hear me. They pushed harder. I was spread-eagled, wind whipping my flying suit so hard it hurt. but I didn't let go. I didn't want to walk back. Finally, they saw the green valley and felt the plane leveling off so a few hands pulled me back in.

My fingers had deep cuts where the sharp aluminum door frame had given me such a good but painful grip. Others were in much worse shape. One pilot had a fork driven deep into his buttocks, another had nasty scalp cuts where he'd broken a ceiling light. Everyone had bruises and minor cuts. Some needed medical attention.

We had run into an embedded thunderstorm – a storm within a large stratus cloud layer – the kind you can't see from inside the clouds. The plane was still flying, both engines running okay but the controls weren't working right. It was flying a little on the diagonal. Subway decided the plane had been damaged structurally and the best bet was to avoid any further stress. We flew in the direction we were headed, west, in the valley, below the clouds and only making gentle turns when the valley wandered.

He had no clear idea where we were except in a valley headed west. We had plenty of gas, about seven hours of flying time left. If we went west far enough, we might be able to get out from under the clouds, fly north to the Wei River then head back east toward Sian.

There were no medical kits in the plane. We had a few small bandages in our parachute seat packs and they were put to use. One of the passengers went into shock; his injuries weren't bad but the wild ride did him in.

After flying west for an hour the overcast started getting higher with a few cracks showing. Just about the time Subway was considering turning north, a small gravel runway came into view. It was located near a village. We couldn't find it on our maps but they were notoriously inaccurate anyway. We circled it. No facilities, taxi strips, wind sock, buildings whatsoever; just a runway about two thousand feet long.

The consensus of opinion was to put her down there. Maybe we could get some medical help and besides, the damn wings could fall off anytime. We landed.

Spontaneous cheers went up when the wheels touched. It seemed like we couldn't get out of the faithful, trusty C-47 fast enough. Several men went down on their knees and kissed the gravel. Curious about structural damage, I walked up under the center section of the wing and started inspecting. Hundreds of rivet heads had been sheared off as the wing spars bent beyond their structural limit. Somehow the wings had stayed together. They were permanently bent but still there. It had been close. I thought about my classmates at Bruning who fell out of the bottom of a thunderhead and formed a respect for thunderstorms that served me well the rest of my flying life. Only luck helped me survive the first one.

We had been on the ground about fifteen minutes when a delegation of people emerged from the village and walked toward the airstrip. It included two Chinese nuns in black habits. We were pleased to find they spoke a little English. Even better, they had medical training and some supplies in their mission. Two of the least banged-up people were assigned first shift guard duty for the plane and the rest of us headed for the village. We'd learned long ago that in China, the only way to avoid having anything and everything stolen was to have American guards.

They were pleased to have visitors. Our landing was the first in almost six months.

Medical procedures were interesting – a blend of 'modern' things such as iodine and gauze bandages with traditional salves and powders from unidentified sources. A few politely declined the less familiar forms. The disturbed, shocked passenger calmed down and we relaxed in peaceful village surroundings.

The big question was, "What happens next?" No one wanted to get back in the bent-winged C-47. We probably had enough fuel to reach Sian if we didn't have too much trouble finding it. Gasoline was dripping off the bottom of the center section. Probably some fuel line connections had been stretched too. My guess was that the leaks didn't amount to more than a quart or two an hour. We had been on a flight plan and our non-arrival would be noticed. Certainly they'd send out some search planes as soon as the weather broke so we decided to just stay there and wait for someone to come and get us.

Food could be a problem but no one in his right mind traveled in China without a few cans of C rations and that all-important staple – American-made toilet paper. The village people, mission staff and Americans pooled their resources and we got along just fine. Most of us slept in the mission buildings on cots, pallets of quilts placed on groups of chairs and on benches.

We were entertained the first night in a most unexpected way. After we'd eaten several people started moving chairs out into a courtyard. Soon groups of villagers began to wander in carrying stools or pillows. A little gasoline generator bolted to a wheelbarrow was wheeled in, then the nuns emerged from a storehouse with a 16mm movie projector and folding screen.

About one hundred people were sitting in front of the screen by sundown. After about ten minutes of cranking with both Americans and Chinese offering advice and tweaking things, the generator started running. No muffler but it didn't make any difference because the American-made movie (I don't remember the name) had Chinese sub-titles and no sound. Watching the audience and their reactions to situations on the screen was much more interesting than the movie.

We were confident that any search plane crew that came within miles of our location would see the C-47 parked on the runway, in plain sight from all directions. The only problem was no one came within miles. Not even distant sound of an airplane reached our ears for three days. The troops were getting restless. Finally group opinion shifted to flying ourselves to Sian.

The next morning was cool, bright, windless and clear. A high pressure area was over us and, if we were ever going to go, this was the time. We thanked our hosts and left all the Chinese money we had (of questionable use out there) and anything else in our possession that they might be able to use, including the beat-up officers' mess kit.

The flight to Sian was smooth and dull. The control tower gave us a green light when we wordlessly entered the landing pattern. An airplane without a working radio wasn't that unusual in China. We taxied to the squadron area and parked close to operations. A few of our buddies were sitting on benches in the shade. They looked our way as we started climbing out, many still wearing bandages supplied by the nuns. You could see their faces light up as they recognized us, then turn to frowns as they couldn't comprehend. Their first comments as they reached us were, "Jesus Christ! Where the hell have you been? Why in hell didn't you let us know where you were? The search was called off. We were sure you had pranged on one of the ridges. We thought you were all dead."

There were elements of both happiness and relief in the situation. They were unhappy because, regardless of intentions, we had caused them grief.

After the war was over we ferried all our planes to Japanese airfields being taken over by Chiang Kai-shek. I was one of a group selected to return to India and fly more brand new P-47s up to Chaing's bases. That trip was my last real adventure of World War II.

Stateside goodies were virtually non-existent in Sian. Our supply line was too long to have any luxuries flown in. The Chinese provided all shelter and food, for a price. Candy bars were rationed – two per month. Absolutely no American beer, fruit juice or wine. Two ounces of stateside whiskey was issued to each pilot after a mission. Our condition when we landed in late August at an air depot near Calcutta could best be described as 'dry.'

Goodies were no longer rationed in India. Hoarded supplies suddenly became surplus as everything was being shut down, closed up, shipped back or destroyed. I heard huge explosions in a depot area every so often; they were getting rid of bombs and new six-by-six trucks at the same time by parking a truck over a bomb then detonating it.

P-47s did not have baggage compartments. Traveling pilots often stuffed clothes and personal items in the eight 50-caliber gun and ammunition compartments within the wings. Someone discovered beer cans fit perfectly in the ammo racks so we started quantity buying. I wasn't a beer-drinker so I bought fruit juice.

The planes we were ferrying did not have belly- or wingtanks so our flights were short, landing in the upper Assam Valley of India and Burma before going over the hump into China. At each base we bought all the beer we could find until the planes were filled. Every P-47 except mine had fourteen cases of beer in its wings when we left Burma. My plane was referred to as the "Fruit Juice Express."

The planes were "new" but had been sitting in the depot for many months without being run. They were in bad shape. No mechanics or parts were available to fix them. Fuel leaks, dead batteries, faulty spark plugs and bad radios plagued us all the way back to Sian. One plane's engine quit just after take-off from a field near Kunming. Mitch, the pilot, wasn't injured and he recovered his beer – but the plane was destroyed.

On the last leg, Chengtu to Sian, we flew high, just to cool the beer. Ice wasn't available in Sian. We'd sent a message ahead to let the troops know what treasure lay within our wings. When we landed, about half of the squadron was standing on the ramp equipped with screw drivers for opening the compartment covers and beer can openers. A significant portion of the beer was gone within thirty minutes.

Between World War II and Korea, I got married, left active duty but accepted a reserve commission and did all sorts of things to make ends meet. A seaplane charter pilot in Puget Sound was my most interesting job but winter was too long and business too slow. I completed a civilian aircraft mechanics course at Dallas Aviation School and later went to Seattle for an interview with Boeing Aircraft Company. They gave me a job as a pre-flight inspector on B-50s. As I came in the door at home, I said, "Pack your bags, honey; we're moving to Seattle." Janice said right back, "You had better read this letter first." It was a notice from the Air Force ordering me to report for a physical; I was being recalled to active duty as a fighter pilot for Korea.

I was soon in the same situation as World War II, trained into a surplus. They had too many fighter pilots and too little fuel in China when I got there. This time, after finishing refresher training in T-28s at a base that shall remain nameless, I learned that there were too many fighter pilots in the personnel pipeline and I had to start looking for a different job. I suggested, with my civilian aircraft mechanic's license, that I go to an aircraft maintenance officers' school. The Air Force liked that idea but I'd have to wait about six months for a class opening. In the meantime, someone decided I was just the person to fix up a little local problem.

It concerned an auxiliary base we'll call Karpal. The runways were heavily used every flying day for B-25 practice landings and take-offs. A staff of about twenty headed by a sergeant were stationed there to man the control tower, several fire trucks and an ambulance. Two cooks took turns feeding them.

The day before I started looking for a temporary job, flight operations were suspended at the auxiliary field because all five trucks and the ambulance were stuck in mud – not on the long gravel road to the base or in the parking lot but out in the middle of the field, between the runways, where none of them should have been.

My first assignment was to find out why and then make damn sure it didn't happen again. Karpal was about ten miles from the nearest paved road. Its angle-iron supported control tower came into view several miles away, confirming that the instructions I'd been given for driving out to it were accurate. It struck me as an odd place for an air base any time, war or peace. I couldn't see the buildings until coming over the last rise. Ugh! All three of them were tar-paper covered, temporary structures, intended to last only as long as World War II. A two-bay crash station sat on the edge of a concrete airplane parking ramp, nestled close to the control tower. A few feet away was a standard 20 by 100 foot barracks. A forest of power poles and scores of bare concrete foundations within a grid of black-top streets told me it had been a busy place at one time.

Toward the north, a motor pool building stood with one of its shed-like side wings hanging down at a crazy angle, indicating wind damage. Farther to the north was a concrete water tower, topped by a wooden tank also tipping at a crazy angle. The area was known as "Tornado Alley" and one had obviously come close to that part of the base.

I turned in the unguarded, sign-less gate and followed tracks in the dirt that lead directly towards the south end of the barracks where a few cars were parked. Some white specks I'd seen in the distance turned out to be chickens, dozens of them. What in the hell were live chickens doing on an Air Force installation – was the main base sending up live meat for the cooks?

A chicken investigation wasn't on my agenda for that day – I wanted to find out how they had managed to get every vehicle stuck at the same time. It was easy. I just introduced myself to Sgt. Shanks, the man in charge and we started talking. He reported that, since there weren't any amusement facilities (bars, girls, etc.) near the base, it had been a common practice to allow the guys to use some of the vehicles for recreation. Hunting was good on the base, a little like an exclusive federal game preserve, so they used the airplane tug to scare up jack rabbits, raccoons and other game. One person would drive the roof-less, windshield-less airplane tug; passengers, sitting on the fenders, would blast away with their shotguns. While chasing a rabbit they plunged deep into a low swamp-like area and became hopelessly stuck. They walked back and drove the pick-up out to rescue the tug but it got stuck too. Next, they tried the four-wheel drive ambulance, then the small crash truck, then the big crash truck, then the humongous Cardox (ten-wheel drive carbon dioxide bottle). A contingent of men and equipment from the main base spent a full day extracting the vehicles.

My orders were clear and simple – the auxiliary base was my responsibility. Anything that happened was on my shoulders. Commuting 120 miles per day in my nine miles per gallon 1947 Buick Roadmaster was economically impossible. Besides, I felt uneasy sleeping that far away from my fate. I rented a furnished farm house near the base ($30 a month) and borrowed an Air Force truck to move my family and few belongings closer to the new job.

The first week was spent getting acquainted with the men and learning more about their work – and play. My conclusion was that duty at Karpal was a hardship – no PX, no movies, terrible living facilities (a one room tar-paper covered barracks, uninsulated, with a single coal stove for heat), and located twelve miles from the nearest town, population 450. Social facilities other than churches or bars were fifty miles away.

A check of records down at the main base told me a lot about why they had a history of personnel problems at Karpal. People at the big base had been using it as a 'Little Siberia.' About half of the men assigned there had been court-martialed within the previous six months. The remainder were deemed misfits or screw-ups and sent out to the auxiliary base just to get rid of them.

Regardless of the reasons for being sent there, I felt these men deserved better treatment. My primary goal became improving quality of life for the group.

The food was bland, to say the least. I asked the cooks to spark up the menu and prepare dishes with appropriate seasonings. They complained that the only seasonings they had were salt and pepper. I phoned the mess sergeant at the main base where they drew their rations and asked him to send out seasonings. The next day we received *nine pounds* of bay leaves, nothing else.

I inventoried the kitchen. There were more than one hundred pounds of butter in the refrigerator, along with several out-of-season ducks. Two large garbage cans were completely filled with fresh ground coffee, about two hundred pounds. It took time to learn why they had been in the habit of ordering so much butter – the owner of a small gas station/food store had a deal with 'the boys at the base':

one pound of butter was worth one pack of cigarettes. The two hundred pounds of coffee went unexplained – it just accumulated.

Tom Stephens made really good chili. I asked him to cook up a batch for lunch one day when we expected an inspection team. It was ready on time and everyone, including the inspectors, trooped into the little dining room we'd made of varnished plywood and sat down to enjoy his specialty. The rich mixture was spicy and, I thought, included more than the usual amount of black pepper. I could see a lot of black flakes in it. The chili was going down fast until someone said, "I don't know about yours but the pepper in my chili has legs." I looked closer. Sure enough, a substantial portion of the meat in the chili was insect life. Personal reactions were interesting. One airman stood up, walked outside and threw up on the new grass. Most, like me, just quit eating. Several men took the attitude that meat is meat and it's all cooked so what the hell, and continued to eat. One went back for seconds.

Our only duty was to man the ambulance, crash trucks and control tower while the B-25s were shooting landings. The barracks was close enough to the crash station to qualify as stand-by area so the entire crew could be used all day every day for self-help work projects.

One of the first things the men wanted was a basketball court next to the crash station. I scrounged hoops, balls and back-stops from the base non-appropriated fund manager but no poles were available. The solution seemed simple: just cut down a couple of the useless power poles scattered around the base and use them. I sent Sgt. Shanks and a squad of men out to pick out two good poles and bring them back. In less than a day we had the basketball court completed. It was used many hours every day and the men became very good basketball players. Later they formed a team that played in local tournaments.

A problem with the basketball court project surfaced when a group of base installations people came up to see what miraculous improvements had been made. They immediately spotted the two former power poles supporting the backstops and hoops. I was escorted to the presence of the poles. Some numbers on them were pointed out to me (I had thought they were of no consequence) and then I received a short course on 'real property installed equipment.' It seemed that every pole is serialized and inventoried just like buildings and every one is located on a map. What I had directed to be done was a crime, unauthorized removal and damage (we'd sawed them off) to government property. My rejoinder was that they weren't doing any good where they had been; they were very useful and appreciated in their new location and, so far as I was concerned, they were going to stay there. If 'corrective action' had to be taken, send me the bill, court martial me or whatever. I told them if their priorities for records and procedures were higher than the men's welfare, I was sorry.

Except for a few comments from my boss and others regarding 'the logging operations at Karpal Air Force Base', I didn't hear any more about them. No bill, no legal actions. I guess someone made appropriate notations somewhere in the volumes of papers stacked in various bureaucrats' offices.

The farm house I rented for my family was typical for the area; no running water, an oil stove, and an outhouse. The phone was a wooden, wall-mounted type that you cranked when you wanted the operator. Later, we learned to dread every time the phone rang our party line signal (three long rings) after dark.

One of the first middle-of-the-night calls we received was to inform me that they had wrecked the pick-up. I drove to the scene of the accident, about half-way between the closest bar and the base. Rain had made the half-gravel, half-dirt road slippery and the truck lay in a ditch on its side. It had rolled over once but not one of the seven people riding in it was hurt bad enough to require medical attention. I had given orders that no more than three could ride in the cab so there must have been four in back. They said that's the way they were riding. This was hard to believe because I had been riding in the back of a Boy Scout truck years before when it rolled. Being thrown from a truck bed is a violent experience; somebody should be hurt. Moreover they were too clean; just muddy shoes.

I said I really wanted to believe them but I just couldn't. They agreed it would have been a miracle (clean and unhurt) – if all seven of them hadn't been in the cab, someone would have been hurt. They were big guys and it was a standard Dodge pick-up with a single bench seat. No wonder no one was hurt; they didn't have room to rattle inside that small cab.

We settled on a story that would hold the men blameless and conform to all regulations. I called the main base the next morning to report the incident, requesting a wrecker and a new pickup. We got them.

Two weeks later I got another call in the early evening; the new pick-up had been wrecked. This time there had been only three people in it and they were going into town – sober. They had met another car at the top of a hill on a narrow gravel road. Each swerved to avoid the other. The light pick-up went out of control in loose sand and rolled.

I called the base. They were very unhappy and launched a full-fledged investigation. Fortunately, everything was right this time. No lies. We got another new pick-up and no punishments.

About two weeks later, the phone rang at 2:00 A.M. It was PFC. Jones calling from a pay phone on a telephone pole near the center of a small town. He said, "Sir, Sims (an airman I'd had trouble with before) has got the ambulance and he's driving like hell all around town with the red light and siren on." In the background, I could hear the siren; it grew louder and completely drowned out Jones' next words. I could also hear the squealing tires as Sims took the corner by the phone at high speed. When we could communicate again, he said two airmen were there with him. I knew Sims got a little violent when he was drunk but three should be able to hold him. I asked him to try to stop Sims, then yank him out of the ambulance and sit on him until I could get more help.

I threw on my clothes and drove to the base. Just as I came in the door the phone rang. It was Jones. He said, "We have Sims."

"How did you get him to stop?"

"It was easy. He hit a light post."

The ambulance was badly damaged but Sims had only scrapes and bruises.

Sims would not settle down so I put him in the back seat of my Buick between two big airmen, drove down to the main base and put him in the stockade.

Next morning, I called for a wrecker and a new ambulance. The call was not well received. About an hour later I was directed to report to the base commander, giving a full account of how I had managed to wreck three vehicles in four weeks.

At last! An opportunity to set things straight for a group of people I felt were being given the short end of the stick! I explained the short-sighted personnel policy of using assignment to the auxiliary base as a punishment, the very poor facilities, lack of adequate transportation, etc. and wound up the meeting by requesting a new eight-seat utility van so the men could ride inside a heavier, better-handling vehicle. I got it.

That afternoon I parked the new carry-all outside the crash station and called a meeting of everyone on the base. My speech was short: "If you want to get rid of me, wreck this vehicle." Six months later, there wasn't a scratch on it.

As the men got more confidence in me, I learned a lot of things about them. Getting rid of the chickens had been easy. I simply said, "Kill and eat the ones that are here and don't bring any more in." They were all gone within a month.

But where had they come from? It was about three months before I learned the whole truth. A woman lived on a farm near there who was past her prime in appearances but definitely still interested in men and sex. There was nothing she liked better than the young virile airmen from the base. They all agreed she was one hell of a hump but you had to have a strong stomach to put up with her house and personal attributes. She realized the men sometimes regarded her as the last choice but her needs were great (sometimes two or three men) so she established a motivational award program. When she was happy with the way things went, she would reward the boys with a few live chickens.

I went to the base one night to take a shower (Janice had to take baths in a washtub at home). Two airmen were standing in front of the urinals using pro kits (prophylactic kits distributed to airmen for reducing the odds of picking up a venereal disease). When they were done, I heard one say, "Now, let's go to town." I wondered what they meant; they must have *been* in town if they were using pros. Then, as I was drying myself, I saw a vehicle leave the crash station, go out on the runway and park.

I asked Sgt. Shanks who was doing what out on the runway. The vague answer was somebody probably hunting, maybe. I had other things to do and left it at that.

A few weeks later I drove over to the base on a Sunday morning just to see how things were going. The guys acted kinda' funny when I came in the door. In an alcove at the end of the barracks, I found a girl wearing nothing but a slip, undoubtedly pulled on in haste. Someone must have seen me drive in and broke up the action.

She was very young; claimed to be 16. She had been in the crash station 'entertaining' the boys the night I came up for a shower and had been on the base several times before. I told her not to come back. If she did, it would be necessary to report her to the police, the last thing I wanted to do. Monday morning I sat all the airmen down for a review of statutory rape laws and penalties. No one knew for sure what they were so I made up some good ones.

One night a group of five airmen went to a bar in a larger town about thirty miles away. An incident occurred involving two of the men, Sanders and McGill, witnessed in part by the other three, that somewhat changed my concept of love.

Sanders and McGill were sitting at the bar. An older man, dressed in bib overalls, worn shirt and farmers' boots struck up a conversation and bought them a couple of beers. After a few minutes of conversation about how tough it was making a living on a farm, he mentioned how the work had affected his health. There was no doubt it had been hard on him. After a while he said it had been a year since he'd been able to 'get it up' and his wife was beginning to complain. Then he identified his wife. She was sitting at a table by herself, a large woman who could have been in her 40's. She looked as though she had done her share of the work too, along with probably raising a few kids.

After a little more conversation, the man said a couple of nice young men like them could really make his wife happy. The men weren't quite sure they were hearing what they thought they were hearing and elected not to react to his observation. Small talk continued through another round while the woman sat by herself, drinking beer and smoking cigarettes.

The nature of the conversation changed abruptly however when the husband said, "Let's go for a ride. I'll bring the wife along and you can take turns screwing her."

They took a closer look at the wife. She was wearing a worn but clean cotton dress and looked younger and prettier as beer and hormones began to influence certain behavior patterns and goal-directed activities in their brains. They looked at each other to confirm their re-directed ambitions, got off their stools and headed over to meet the wife.

All of them sat down and drank another round of beers while they talked about the crops, weather and war. When the glasses were empty, the husband stood and suggested they take a ride to cool off a little. The other airmen observed the beer buying, the move to the table and then out the door, but not having heard the conversations, wondered what was going on.

The car was a big old Hudson that had seen better days. He got behind the wheel; the wife climbed in back, sat in the middle and patted the seat on each side of her. They headed out of town on a gravel road. The airmen didn't know what was expected or what to do so they just sat there. After a few minutes of riding, she took things into her own hands, literally. She advised the boys there was no point in being bashful, then assigned their hands to her huge breasts (they said it took two hands to hold one) while she worked on their zippers. By the time they pulled into an area that looked like an abandoned gravel pit and stopped, she had the full attention of both men.

The husband got out and walked back behind the car. She squeezed both penises, perhaps judging their hardness and/or size (they didn't ask) then asked McGill to go outside and wait a few minutes.

Despite the Hudson's generous back seat area, effective lovemaking required both doors to be open. The husband and McGill made small talk, electing not to discuss the interior activity until seat springs began squeaking rhythmically. As the intensity increased, to the obvious satisfaction of the husband, he jabbed McGill and said, "Damn! He's giving her a good ride, ain't he?"

Shortly after the squeaking stopped, Sanders walked towards the men, zipping his pants and said, "She wants you right now."

When McGill had done his best to make her happy, she followed him out of the car. The three men were lighting cigarettes while she opened the trunk lid and began rummaging around in the dark interior. Finally she located everything she wanted – a bottle of Coca-Cola and an opener. After hiking her skirt up around her generous hips, she squatted in the road, pressed her thumb over the opened Coca-Cola, shook it vigorously then pushed the end into her vagina.

Next morning, the men were comparing observations and impressions about the incident with a group of interested listeners (including me). One man's conclusion was interesting in a very basic way – he was never going to drink another Coke from a bottle. I concluded initially that they were simply a couple with unique sexual habits. Years later, my opinion changed. I saw it as an incident driven by a sincere desire to fulfill the other person's needs. The act could have been an expression of love.

We attended a six-man high school football game one Friday night. The local barber came up to me as we were walking towards the small spectator stands and said, "Honest, Lieutenant, I didn't want to do it. They made me!"

"Made you do what?"

His jaw dropped far enough to put his foot in his mouth as he had just done and then he said, "My God! You haven't seen them yet." He turned around and walked away shaking his head.

By then Janice and I had grown thick skins regarding surprises so we didn't pursue the barber for more information – what will be will be. As we stepped onto the cinder track around the field, we saw a group of our airmen with several young girls around them, all in animated conversation. The objects of much pointing, laughing and touching were their heads, decorated with pheasant tail feathers and decidedly non-regulation Mohawk haircuts.

One of the guys spotted us and said something to them. Two of them acted embarrassed. The rest had drunk too many beers to care. I waved to the group and smiled. They were having fun and nothing official would have to happen before Monday. By then, after a few looks in a mirror, I figured it wouldn't take much persuasion to get the rest of their heads shaved.

Saturday morning I drove to the base and asked the five men still there that had Mohawks if I could take their picture. They were acting sheepish. I didn't feel it was necessary to make any comments regarding their stupidity. However, curiosity got the better of me and, after taking several pictures, I asked how the new hair-do movement got started. They had been drinking beer in the bar next to the barber shop late Friday afternoon. Sims got the idea that getting a Mohawk hair-cut would be an excellent example of discipline rejection (his words were more likely along the line of "fuck the Air Force") and volunteered to get the first one if everyone in the group would commit to getting their hair cut the same way. They agreed and headed next door.

When Sims stepped out of the barber's chair, the balance of the group attempted to renege on their vows – he looked ridiculous. Sims was not to be denied; his tendency towards violence was known and he threatened to beat the shit out of anyone who didn't get his Mohawk. They got them.

Monday morning there were no Mohawks in sight but the casual observer might have thought a group of Buddhists had taken over the airport.

My school assignment finally came through and we left for Chanute AFB, IL. About seven months later the Air Force sent us to Guam. My assignment was aircraft maintenance officer and pilot for the 79th Air Rescue Squadron. Its stated mission was to accompany B-29 bombers going to and from Korea. Our planes were SB-29s, converted bombers which had large lifeboats slung beneath them. The gasoline engine powered aluminum boat could be dropped by parachute to a crew in the water. We flew a few missions over Korea but, like my World War II duty, the hot action was over before I got there.

Much to my surprise, I was offered a regular Air Force commission after my duty on Guam. I liked the wide variety of planes I'd been flying and the financial security looked good to Janice so I signed on the dotted line. What followed was mostly a series of staff jobs within SAC. My one operational assignment between Korea and Vietnam was as maintenance supervisor of a Titan I missile squadron. After two years of 'hiding' underground, hoping the wheels in SAC Headquarters would forget me, a telegram came in reassigning me to staff work again – this time at SAC Headquarters.

Chapter 2

THE PUZZLE PALACE

The halls at Strategic Air Command Headquarters (SAC) were long green tunnels with polished floors. I had been trudging through them almost four years, carrying inconsequential papers or headed for meetings with little significance. The book title "Treadmill to Oblivion" came to mind often in those surroundings. It seemed as if the Air Force was determined to keep me doing what I didn't want to do: staff work.

There I was, a 43-year-old lieutenant colonel with white hair and a long record of staff jobs. My next assignment was almost sure to be the Pentagon, where the halls were darker and truly endless. Worse yet, about five years back, the Air Force had taken me off active flight status. My career had turned from one of travel, variety and adventure to bureaucratic drudgery.

My destination one morning in December of 1966 was a door with a super-secret warning sign on it. The little plastic badge on my uniform had the appropriate punches so I could open the door and walk in with a qualified degree of impunity. Inside I met another officer/bureaucrat in a cubbyhole just large enough for two straight chairs and a mini-desk. While we were deeply engrossed in a conversation of no consequence, the door popped open and Pete Jones, my office buddy, stuck his head in. His face showed concern. He said, "Brownie, guess what! You're going to Vietnam. You're going to be a forward air controller."

I was a little surprised. After two wars with combat missions in both and then inactive flying status, I hadn't considered drawing a combat flying assignment in Vietnam.

I thought, "Those bastards in Personnel have done it to me again." They waited for my reaction. We'd all been surprised by orders like this before. It was interesting to see how people reacted to abrupt changes in their lives and plans. Then it hit me: Hey, I'm outta' here; I'm outta' these God-damned cubbyholes; I'm back in the air where I can make decisions and see different things; I'm free! I think I smiled.

Pete said, "I know a guy in Personnel that can probably get you off the list." I thought about the Pentagon and said, "Don't try."

The 'list' was a roster of older, inactive pilots who were to be given refresher flight training and sent to combat assignments in Vietnam. Most of the pilots were like me, World War II and/or Korea types with just a few years (in my case, one and a half) before being eligible for retirement. Did the people in Personnel have a special meaning in mind when they named the project 'Palace Gate'?

The retreads were given a variety of flying jobs. Some were assigned to fly C-123s, small cargo planes used for carrying supplies to combat bases and hauling loads of bodies to the mortuaries at larger bases. Others flew gun ships such as Spookys, which were C-47s equipped with high speed Gatling guns that fired out the side. It appeared that anyone with fighter experience (22 years back in my case) became a forward air controller.

The piston engined fighters of World War II and the jets of 1966 had little in common except their missions: shoot down aircraft, strafe and bomb ground targets. During Korea, they discovered jets burned fuel so fast at low altitude and their turning radius was so large (because of speed) that it was darned near impossible for the pilots to accurately locate ground targets in the time available. T-6 trainers from World War II were pressed into service. They carried target marking rockets that produced large puffs of white smoke where they hit and a variety of radios with ground troop, control center, and aircraft frequencies. Their function was to find targets and mark them for the fighters. Pilots who flew the T-6s were called Forward Air Controllers (FACs).

FACs were flying O-1s in Vietnam. They consisted of the wings and tail surfaces of the popular Cessna 170-B, a four-seat private type aircraft, with a special two-seat fuselage and larger engine. It had big windows, many radios and self-sealing tanks. It didn't have bullet-proof glass, armor or extra engines, things that were nice to have in combat.

For me, it was a lucky break. I'd always enjoyed light, simple airplanes, owning and flying them since going on inactive duty at the end of World War II. Now I could fly the type of airplanes I liked and get paid for it. Fringe benefits to my Palace Gate nomination were escape from staff work, SAC and the Pentagon.

There was no escape from telling my wife Janice, however. I picked up a little more information about my new job, continued working and went home at the usual time, trying to be casual. She was accustomed to surprise announcements that took me away from her and the two boys for periods of days to months. This one was received a little differently.

Janice knew I disliked my staff job but regular hours and less frequent traveling had given her a taste of security that she was reluctant to lose. After I answered some 'when and where' questions, Janice sat there a few minutes. I could see it was hitting her hard. She would have the two boys (now teenagers) to raise for a year, she would be sleeping in the same bed, only alone, she would have to manage the household, she would have the worry, the fear of what was happening to me on the other side of the earth. She said, "I don't feel like cooking tonight. Let's go eat someplace." The mood was somber during the meal. In fact, the atmosphere at our table was so dismal it was fifteen years before I could get her to go back to that restaurant.

Things started happening fast. All Palace Gate pilots in SAC headquarters were called together the next day for a briefing. I learned we'd be given flight refresher training right there at Offutt, my home base. It would consist of nothing more than a few hours in an instrument flight simulator, some flying time then stand-board and instrument flight check rides. Luck was with me again when I was assigned to 'Blue Canoes' (U-1s) for flying time. They were good airplanes, military versions of the Cessna 310, a light twin engine civil aircraft. I had admired them for years and only regretted that I'd have so little time for flying. The agenda after refresher flight training was full. There would be very little time at home between then and April, when I was due in Vietnam. Most of February and March would be spent at Hurlburt Field, Eglin AFB, down on the Gulf Coast, in FAC training. Late in March I'd be taking survival training at Fairchild AFB, near Spokane, Washington. Jungle survival training in the Philippines would be my last stop, early in April, on the way to Vietnam.

My arrival at Hurlburt Field was like a bad dream. I didn't mention the experience to anyone until long after leaving the place. It was about 11:00 P.M. The cab driver was willing but inexperienced and had never driven on the base before. A guard at the gate gave us directions to the Bachelor Officers' Quarters (BOQ) registration office, next to the Officers' Club. Minutes later, we were lost. We came to some buildings identified as BOQs but the registration office wasn't there. Just beyond the end of the BOQ area the road came to a dead end. We stopped to discuss our next move.

The area was grass covered and reasonably flat with a few pine trees scattered around. I could see a large, lighted building some distance off to the right. Music was coming from the building and I decided it had to be the Club. He said, "Let's go!" I assumed he'd circle back around the large open area but that wasn't his plan. Instead, he cramped the wheel around, bounced over the curb and headed across the grass, directly towards the big building.

I sat in back, hoping we wouldn't hit any alligators and mildly curious about the little hills we were going around and over. He was really moving. We did a zero-gravity over one hill and came crashing down on a flat area – then I knew where we were. A slender white mast with a red triangular flag went by the window. We were on the golf course and had just crossed a green.

Somehow we got to a parking lot on the dark side of the Club, dropped down to the good old pavement and drove up to the registration office just like everyone else. No sirens, no MPs. The next day I couldn't even look at the golf course. Luckily, I don't play.

Aside from the karate instructor who kept making us old pilots do deep knee bends until we were nearly crippled, the experience at Hurlburt was pleasant.

Airplanes with tail wheels require different landing and taxi techniques than those with the third wheel under the nose. They are more sensitive to cross-winds and have a tendency to ground-loop (out-of-control turns) since the center of gravity is behind the front, non-steering wheels. Most ground-loops are only embarrassing. My worst was one dark and stormy night on Iwo Jima. As I turned off the runway, the C-47 decided to do a 360 degree right turn before continuing. The squadron commander was in the right seat and there were about ten pilots in the back end. Every one of them felt it necessary to give me some advice on flying tail-wheel equipped airplanes. I blamed it on a weak left brake but no one believed me.

The Cessna O-1 has a tail wheel.

For me, the first day of flying was fun. My years of experience in light planes paid off. Some of the re-treads hadn't flown a tail-wheel airplane or anything smaller than a B-25 since World War II. I stood out on the ramp and watched the light, responsive O-1s being grossly over-controlled by pilots accustomed to grunt-and-groan controls. Taxi and take-off headings varied up to forty-five degrees. There were a few scuffed wing-tips and bent propellers but all the O-1s and the pilots in my class survived the re-adjustment period.

My instructor had just returned from Vietnam. Check-out consisted of a familiarization flight around the huge Eglin test range and outlying auxiliary flight strips then back to Holly. My landing apparently was satisfactory. He told me to take the airplane out to one of the strips and practice landings or whatever until I had the specified amount of flying time.

In just a few hours I learned to love the O-1, particularly the O-1E version. It had a large fixed pitch propeller that gave the plane excellent acceleration and climb performance. Straight and level flying felt like driving in second gear but no one who needed to go somewhere very far away would pick an O-1.

The planes used for transition training were light-weights. They didn't have a full set of radios or carry any rockets. In that configuration and solo, the O-1s were hot rods. Take-offs occurred almost instantly. Climbs were steep and descents even steeper, thanks to huge wing flaps that came down to a sixty degree angle. Take-off, climb, turn down-wind, turn at the end of the runway, land and stop took less than one minute.

Forward Air Controller training consisted of a lot of ground school and less flying than I wanted. Reading military maps was a major subject. We had to be able to pin-point the location of objects on the ground using nothing but the maps and grid coordinates. Man-made things such as buildings, roads, bridges plus ground contour (shown by lines on the maps), vegetation, lakes and rivers were used as reference points. Sometimes, radio navigation aids for aircraft could be used as cross references. Imagine the consequences of reading a map incorrectly when calling for artillery to help someone on the ground.

Wrong coordinates could waste time or, even worse, kill the friendlies. Our map reading final tests came in the air when we had to fly to and identify certain objects, some as small as an oil drum, when given only map coordinates, and then develop accurate coordinates for objects selected by the instructor.

After controlling two practice air strikes (one dual, one solo) on the Eglin bomb range, I was deemed ready to go – a qualified FAC.

The basic job was simple: when a need for air support had been established, the FAC called someone to send out what was needed, giving his location with a radio fix (so many miles out on a certain radial of a navigational radio system) or a large, easy-to-see geographical feature (a mountain, large bay, etc.). When the fighters arrived, he briefed the pilots on their proper heading into and away from the target, where the friendlies (if any) were, what to expect in the way of hostilities, and a few other details. When everything was ready, he would roll into a dive and fire a 'Willy-Pete' (white phosphorous) marking rocket at the target.

The FAC would make a quick break to one side as soon as the rocket was on its way and get into position to see where it hit. If he was lucky, he'd tell the first aircraft to "hit my smoke" or something like "one hundred meters left" if he wasn't. He or the friendly people on the ground would judge the effectiveness of the ordnance after each release. Re-marking the targets or giving verbal adjustments to the fighter pilots before each pass allowed 'fine tuning' impact points to meet needs. A more detailed description of a FAC's job and responsibilities is in Appendix B.

One of the things that bothered me at first was the lack of any type of an aiming system for the smoke rockets. Some pilots made grease pencil marks on the windshield according to a variety of rules but none of them helped me. What seemed to work best was simply flying straight towards the target, keeping it steady in the windshield until, when prudence won out over guts, you fired the rocket and broke away. In the age of computers, radar, sophisticated aircraft gun sights, we were marking targets with rock-throwing techniques. They worked remarkably well and not one FAC mission in O-1s was lost because of a rocket sight malfunction.

Two Palace Gate pilots who had been sent to C-123 training at Eglin talked the school into scheduling a 'navigation' training mission to Offutt over a weekend. They could leave Saturday morning and had to have the plane back by 6:00 P.M. Sunday. The word was passed around and about ten more Palace Gaters were in the back end when they took off.

I didn't know how slow a 123 would go. Turbulence, head winds, anxiety and cold made the flight miserable. It was dinnertime before I got home. We talked, ate home cooking and the boys went back to their hobbies and studies. I gave Janice a passionate embrace and started for the bedroom. She gave me a "regrets" look and said she was sorry but it was just the wrong time of the month.

Sunday morning I walked towards the C-123 through wind and snow, dreading the long flight back and damning everything in sight.

Chapter 3

LIVING THROUGH IT

Survival training was not a requirement for my previous flying duties in SAC since I hadn't been on a combat crew. The moaning and groaning and horror stories I had heard from my friends after going through the school convinced me that it was to be avoided if at all possible. Now fate had caught up with me and at the tender age of 43, I was going to see if all those stories were true or just B.S. The weather in the school area, northern Washington, at that time of the year also gave me concern.

Students had to run any time they were outside and moving towards any destination – no walking except in buildings. After a few days of running between classes, running to the mess hall, running to the PX, etc., I was ready to do anything so long as it didn't involve more running. I got my wish. The class was given an opportunity to crawl.

Much of the land in that area of Washington has volcanic rock out-croppings – sharp, black lava cliffs, boulders and basalt columns protruding from a thin layer of soil and fine native grasses. Areas that can't be farmed because of rocks are generally for sale, cheap. Naturally, that's where the Air Force would locate its Escape and Evasion training area. It was about a mile long and a few hundred yards wide. Inside the fenced area were all sorts of 'enemy' lookouts, trip-wires attached to flares, barbed wire, various obstacles, and roaming sentries, plus millions of sharp rocks. The objective was to make the distance, at night, without tripping any flares or being caught by the sentries. Penalties were blank shots in your direction, the embarrassment of being illuminated by a brilliant flare while an instructor chewed on you and the threat of failing the course and doing it all over again.

Old hands said the course will kill your knees if you don't protect them. Some had come prepared with thick sponge and tape. Those caught unprepared, like myself, were looking for help. The word went around that ladies' sanitary napkins made good knee pads. I ran over to the little PX on the school grounds to see what was available. To my surprise, it had a large stock of napkins. I bought a box of the heavy duty kind and a sewing kit. Back in the room, I sewed two napkins inside each leg of my pants. The pants puckered and bulged in odd places but a trial crawl down the hall showed me they were in the right positions and surprisingly comfortable. When we assembled that night, I noticed that about half the students had gone the Kotex route. It was a windy, moonless, cold night.

Flare trip-wires were the big problem. Moving slowly on hands and knees, feeling ahead was the only way to be sure. When you found one, the problem was to get over it without standing up. I touched one with my toe. As soon as the wire went slack, I knew there would be trouble. The flare grenade popped and, as light began to flood the area, I saw an instructor/sentry standing ten feet away. In my fatigued, pained state, the most intelligent statement I could come up with was "Oh, shit." He gave me some choice guidance then I sat there, resting, until the light went out.

The rocks were awful. My hands were scratched and bleeding. My pants wore through at the knees and the pads were in shreds before I made it to the end. At that point we were 'captured' by enemy forces, instructors who were very good actors dressed in another nation's uniforms. As prisoners, our treatment was just what we could expect, *not* according to the Geneva Convention.

The escape course had taken many pain-filled hours and what followed was tough – some candidates broke down, cried, revolted, wanted out. Things got terse as soon as we were captured. People were tired and sore. Interrogations, line-ups, harassment, mild physical and psychological torture continued for many hours. We had no watches and the building was windowless. All concept of time was lost.

One routine was particularly bad for those with claustrophobic tendencies. They pushed 'prisoners' into adjustable wooden boxes, forced them into a squatting position and then the top, sides and ends were shoved tightly against their bodies so they couldn't move. When I figured out what was happening, I made myself as large as possible, not bending over completely and spreading my knees. They pushed hard but I pushed hard too. They left when they were satisfied my box was as small as it could be. I waited a few minutes because there were air holes and they might see movement, then I rocked forward onto my sore knees, put my head against the end of the box and tried to sleep. They were busy stuffing other boxes. The noise and commotion was interesting. One guy, who must have had claustrophobia, revolted. He yelled, "There's no way you can put me in that box!" After the 'guards' screamed at him for a while, they decided he was serious. Play time was over. He was taken away.

Later, they locked me into a very small cubicle with my hands tied behind my back and a black hood over my head. I was instructed to make no sounds and remain standing until someone came for me. It was eerie. For a while I killed time designing things, then my fantasies got too real. I concentrated on the realities of the day or night, whatever, until I heard the sound of someone who wasn't taking things too seriously, snoring. That helped me decide that I'd had enough sensory deprivation, sat down in a corner and tried to make a snoring duet. The guard caught me trying to get to my feet when he opened the door. He raised hell but I knew he couldn't shoot me.

After what seemed like days (actually only one), we were released into a prisoner of war compound and left, for the most part, to fend for ourselves. The ranking officer did as he should: set up a prisoner organization, assigned barracks and made a list of requirements for presentation to the prison commander of such things as bedding, toilet paper and food. Escape attempts were planned. It had been about thirty-six hours since we had eaten so food was important. I was appointed the task of getting food. After several arguments and delays, we were issued meat, onions, potatoes, etc. for making a stew. A big pot was located and a wood fire started. After hours of smelling the stew cooking, we were really ready to eat. The prison commander lined us up for chow, made a great speech about how kind his government was, tasted the stew to "insure we were getting the best", spat it out, said, "This is TERRIBLE!" and kicked the pot over. We never did get the bedding or toilet paper.

At one time, the ranking officer was put in solitary confinement for some infraction and I became the leader. The prison camp staff was intimidating, uncooperative and corruptible – very good actors and believable situations.

During one major altercation between prisoners and guards (an attempted escape), I was required to read to all prisoners a prepared statement that violated Geneva Conventions. I refused. That was a mistake. My punishment for screwing up was not a 'D' for the course. Instead, they pushed me into a little 'dog house' about three feet by six feet that had been half filled with rocks about the size of cannon balls. It had been hours since I had sat down so the rocks felt surprisingly soft. I found a relatively comfortable position and thoroughly enjoyed my rest period. Pain is relative.

No school could fully prepare a person to withstand the torture and ill treatment given to our men in the Hanoi Hilton, Bataan Death March or other places. That's up to individual capability. The prisoner part of survival training convinced me that extreme risks and pain were better than capture. Back in China during World War II, we carried a Colt forty-five in a shoulder holster on missions, usually with just one clip of bullets. The first six bullets were for shooting Japanese, the last one was for yourself. When capture by the Japanese was imminent, you had two choices, death by your own hand or torture then death by bayonet or Samurai sword.

As soon as our prison episode was completed, we were given an hour to get our gear together then move on to the next phase: Escape and Evasion, Part Two.

Several school bus loads of tired troops were driven into the mountains north of Spokane and handed rations equivalent to five hundred calories a day for, I think, four days. Part of the rations consisted of live rabbits.

Divided into groups about the size and personnel mix of an aircraft crew, we spent the first night in semi-prepared camp sites with parachutes stretched between trees for shelters. We were so hungry that killing the rabbit and getting it into a stew presented no problem at all. Thinking about the days behind and ahead, we put every edible part of that rabbit in the pot. The guys that got to eat the eyes said they were a little salty.

The night was cold, well below freezing. Each person had two mummy type sleeping bags. The idea was to stuff one inside the other, then stuff yourself inside the inside one, zip it up most of the way then zip up the outside one, then the inside a little more and so on until just your nose was exposed. The only problem was that my arms and hands were held tightly by the bags. Sometime during the first night I rolled off my little pad of pine boughs and woke up face down and almost smothered by the layers of padding. I lost control for a few seconds; I couldn't get my hands up to open the bags and couldn't roll back face up. Finally I calmed down enough to squirm onto one side and get one hand up to the inside zipper. After that experience, I left the top open and covered my face with clothing.

Next morning there was more on-the-scene training in signaling search aircraft and stuff like that. By nightfall, we were as ready as we would ever be for the most arduous part of the survival course: escape and evasion in rough country over long distances.

Rations were carefully divided. I got a couple of pemmican bars and one big onion. We made up back-packs using parachute parts. Mine weighed about twenty-five pounds and contained the two sleeping bags, a shelter half (a large waterproof cloth), an assortment of survival gear, my rations and a canteen. The crews were each given a compass and a map with an 'X' where we had to get to by nightfall. We left at dawn. Routes were optional but walking on or near any of the few roads in the area was strictly forbidden. Besides, they were patrolled by 'hostile forces' and, if captured, we'd get to take the course over again.

I don't know how far it was, some said twenty-five miles, some guessed fifteen, but it was the roughest walking, most arduous exertion I ever experienced. One time we were in waist-deep snow. Some hills were so steep we had to climb on all fours. Our crew stuck together, helped and encouraged each other. Luck was with us on the choice of route and we were among the first crews to the rendezvous point. Never before or since have I felt such fatigue. I wanted to make up a pine bough pad but the exertion of cutting off one branch with my knife was almost too much. After taking a short rest, I bit off a chunk of pemmican and tried to chew it. Too tired, I just swallowed it whole, then waited for the promised surge of energy. None came.

In the last dim light of day, I cut off a few small boughs, said to hell with it and pulled myself into the bags. Frozen ground and twigs can feel real good under those conditions.

Breakfast at dawn consisted of pemmican (now I could chew it) and onion. I found that a small bite of each, chewed together, tasted all right.

We were given maps showing where buses would pick us up the next day, then told to scatter and get there without being captured.

The terrain was terrible – heavily wooded mountains, ravines, wide and sometimes treeless valleys laced with logging and fire roads. Fatigue pressured me to take easy routes but 'enemy forces' patrolled the roads, trails and any place travel was convenient.

Map reading and just plain thinking became difficult. Capture became an acceptable alternative to climbing another hill until I remembered interrogation. Every once in a while I would meet another 'escapee' and exchange information on routes and experiences. An over-weight Palace Gate pilot was having problems – vomiting every few minutes and so weak he staggered. I told him to head for a road and get picked up. "No God-damned training is worth killing yourself," I told him. He said he'd make it, and he did.

About noon the next day, I figured I was only a few miles from the bus pick-up point. There was a road in the valley below me, running along the edge of the woods. A sergeant who had been in my crew during the early part of the training was walking with me. If we were on the road, could we make it into the woods and hide before anyone patrolling in a vehicle could get to where we were? It was worth the risk. Both of us were dead tired, hungry and wanted to be in the first bus to fill and leave for the base.

Down from the ridge and onto the road we went. Never had gravel felt so good. I was confident that we could hear any vehicle coming and get off the road before being seen. We caught up with two men walking in the woods about a hundred feet back from the road. They yelled to us that they hadn't seen any vehicles lately. I invited them down to join us on the road but they declined. Road walking was strictly forbidden.

About two minutes later, surprise! A blue Air Force pick-up came around the curve behind us, moving quite fast, and I heard the throttle go to wide open the second we were seen. Our objective was to be motionless by the time the truck stopped, so both of us dove into the first low spots we could find in the woods. I found a place under a fallen tree, squirmed down as low as I could get, flicked leaves and twigs over me and covered my face. I heard the truck skid to a stop, doors open and men running into the woods. The two more cautious 'escapees' behind us apparently didn't hide very well. They were captured. I lay there and listened while they insisted that they hadn't been down on the road. The guards started to search again, coming within a few feet of us, but our luck held. Finally the guards hauled them away. We resumed our walk but stayed away from the road until the last mile or so from the buses.

It had been days since we'd seen soap or tooth brushes; wearing sweaty, filthy clothes. A diet of pemmican and raw onions didn't help. I smelled so bad myself that a collective estimate of true stench on that bus was impossible. I watched out the back window as we went through Spokane and thought I saw several people on the down-wind side of the street visibly flinch after we went by.

Back home for one last time before the big trip my Air Force-provided check list of things to take was complete. A new last will and testament made and filed; a wash and wear suit; a rain coat; a tape recorder and spare tapes for verbal correspondence.

My last Saturday at home happened to be on the night our square dance club met. I wanted to go because I liked to dance but, better yet, the women would probably give me good-bye hugs. They did, but only a few of the usual bunch went across the street to the bar after the dance. Only a half-hour later, we got the last good-byes from our closest friends and drove home. I mentioned to Janice how few stayed. She said, "Good-byes are painful; they probably didn't want to prolong the agony."

I noticed there were an unusual number of cars parked on the street as we approached our house. Inside, all the lights were on, the rest of the club was there. The wonderful friends who had faked the good-byes at the bar followed us in, ready to give me a send-off I'd always remember. What a party and what a wonderful bunch of people. Friends make life easier.

My last stop before Vietnam was at Clark AFB in the Philippines for jungle survival training. It was a good, well-run school that taught skills very pertinent to the hazards involved in combat flying over jungle. Many pilots survived because of what they learned there.

We traveled by helicopter into a hilly jungle clearing west of Clark after a few days of classroom work. The instructor led us on an orientation walk while describing specific evasion techniques then told me to get going. He'd send the rest of the class out to look for me in exactly five minutes – like hide-and-seek only the stakes later could be higher. I found a clump of bushes with a dark interior, crawled in, lay down in a curled position, threw debris over my body, folded both arms over my head to cover the white hair, then relaxed. It was amazing. I could hear the hunters all around me. One even came up to the clump of bushes I was in and pushed the leaves apart but didn't see me. After about a half hour of searching, the instructor yelled for me to stand up. Several men were within fifty feet.

We spent the first night as a group in a semi-prepared camp site, somewhat like the one in Washington. Beds were platforms made of branches lashed together, suspended a few feet off the ground between tree trunks. The night was pitch black. You really couldn't see your hand in front of your face.

After finishing our C-ration evening meals, the group gathered under a banana-leaf-roofed shelter a previous class had built up against the side of an almost vertical cliff. Someone started a fire for light and anti-mosquito smoke. We sat around the fire and talked, a mixture of horror stories and jokes, to remind ourselves of how brave we were and delay bedtime as much as possible. After a couple of hours, we were running out of good material so even those with no talent, such as I, were afforded speaking time. In desperation, I dug up the old "shark infested custard" riddle (what is soft, yellow and very deadly?). Just as I delivered the punch line there was a tremendous crash, the entire shelter disintegrated and the fire exploded into a million sparks. After hours of scary talk, the sudden violence shattered everyone's last vestige of security. Expletives filled the air, bodies were running into each other and trees. Thumps, bangs and grunts echoed through the black jungle night long after the crash. Gradually people found their flashlights and beams of light started moving around the area. We gathered back at the now flattened shelter. Some men were still shaking. Formerly basso-profundo voices tended toward alto ranges. Smoke filtered up through the pile of banana leaves that had been the roof.

There, lying in the middle of the wreckage was the remains of an old, rotten banana tree; up at the top of the cliff, some fifteen or twenty feet above us, was a spot of freshly torn earth right on the edge. We remembered a dead banana tree had been standing there. It couldn't have picked a more impressive time or direction to return to the earth from which it sprang. No one there will ever forget it.

After that grand finale, sleep did not come quickly. We had been told not to let any part of our bodies touch the mosquito netting. Rat bites, not mosquitoes, were the reason. I could hear them scurrying around, looking for food. Also, the sounds of leaves, twigs, branches and what-have-you as they fell from the upper canopy, a hundred or more feet above us, caused a little apprehension. You could hear them coming – click, whap, rustle, then thud as they hit the soft jungle floor. I lay under the netting wondering if the next one would get me.

Next morning each student was given a map and three metal tags. The map had an 'X' on it, marking where a helicopter would pick him up, using the rope, sling and winch technique, about noon the following day. Each tag was worth one kilo of rice when turned in to the Air Force by local negritos. They were to be the enemy forces for this escape and evasion exercise. Born and raised in the jungle, they would be tough to hide from. We had to give a tag to any negrito who found us after sunset. Woe be unto any student who lost all his tags.

Another Palace Gate FAC pilot, Harry Longfellow, and I had become friends during training. We decided to team up in spite of different objectives. I wanted to play the hide-and-go-seek game. Harry's goal was avoiding the four-legged enemy, rats. We located a big banyan tree with wide-spread roots on a ridge across a valley from the pick-up point. One pair of roots formed a solid 'V' with the ground. Harry planned to keep a fire going all night at the top of the V, with us taking turns sleeping. I complained that we'd lose all our tags for sure. He said, "So what? I'm in no hurry to get to Vietnam anyway." I couldn't argue with that logic.

We finished eating our C-rations and threw the cans over the side of the ridge. They didn't stop moving for fifteen minutes as rats fought for the right to lick them clean. Sounds of the cans being pushed around was great motivation for gathering a supply of fire wood.

It still bugged me. I didn't want to give up on trying to keep my tags so, after the fire was going, I asked Harry if he'd mind too much if I moved away from the tree a little distance to see how good the negritos were at the game. I said I'd be back before midnight and keep the fire going while he slept. My equipment consisted of a shelter-half, a flashlight and a bottle of mosquito repellent. A low narrow trail penetrated the brush straight out from the root-formed V we were in. After going about thirty or forty feet, I came to a place where growth was so thick it was difficult to leave the trail or stand up. Most plants had long stems, about pencil sized, that arced over each other like berry bushes. They were brittle and broke easily so I started off through them, breaking only the minimum necessary. After getting completely off the trail, I reached back and stuck the broken ends in the ground.

I'd gone about twenty-five feet when I came to an area where growth wasn't quite as dense and the ground was soft, almost fluffy. It looked like a good place to sit. One of the first things that caught my eye as I checked the surroundings was ant traffic. It was just like those 'city of the future' drawings I'd seen many times, the kind where tall buildings are connected by skyways with robotic vehicles going every which way. Ants were using those long arced stems as skyways and traffic was intense. Some chugged along the stems like little old ladies, others were going like teenagers in super-charged Corvettes. Occasionally, they stopped head-to-head and did their programming bit of hitting each other's antennae in some routine known only to ants.

At intersections where stems touched and crossed, the ants went different ways. Some would go left, some right, some straight ahead. The thought hit me, what would happen if these programmed insects couldn't follow their instructions? I pulled out my bottle of super insect repellent and dosed one intersection.

Man! What a traffic jam. In seconds there were twenty or thirty ants piled up around the intersection. After much pushing and shoving in very human-like ways, they went to subroutines of some sort and used other skyways. The word got out to other ants and soon traffic up to the dosed intersection dropped off.

I decided to create a New York-type jam by putting insect repellent on every intersection I could reach. It was awful. Some were trapped, going back and forth between intersections, others piling up as alternate routes were blocked. A few took a 'to hell with it' attitude and bolted across the smelly stuff to complete their missions. One of the hot rods did a classic double-take – going so fast that he was across the intersection before noticing something was wrong, then jamming on the brakes, turning around and going back to check the phenomenon he'd sensed. After waving his antenna around for a few seconds, it was off to the races again.

After a while, I found out why the area was open and the ground soft – I was sitting in the middle of a large rat colony. In the dim light I could see dozens of them looking at me. My presence had thrown a monkey wrench into their evening activities. I spread out my shelter-half, sat in the middle of it then pulled the edges up over my head and knees.

Just about the time I was reviewing my decision to hide out, I heard voices coming up the side of the ridge. Two negritos passed close to me on a trail I hadn't noticed and went directly up to Harry. He gave them a friendly greeting and, he said later, handed them one tag. They didn't like that. They indicated with sign language they wanted two tags. Harry said no. There was a lot of talking between them which neither of us could understand then the younger one said very carefully, "Where colonel?" The jungle telegraph was working. Harry said he pointed straight up into the tree. They politely walked all around the tree, carefully inspecting the trunk even though climbing it was impossible. Then they split and started searching for me in earnest. One came down the same trail I had but missed my turn-off point, probably because of the replaced stems.

More people came by to collect tags and Harry paid. Traffic dropped after he ran out of them.

The rats were getting brave. A few of them would charge, turn around when they got close and kick dirt on me. Later, they'd bounce off me as if they were demonstrating clout or trying to push me away. The one thing I didn't want was a bite. A rat-bite meant the Pasteur anti-rabies series of shots, a painful 21-day treatment. I kicked or swatted at any rat that touched me for more than a second. Maybe a rat couldn't bite through the shelter-half but I didn't feel like giving one the opportunity to prove it could.

About 11:00 I rejoined Harry and spent the night by the side of the fire. I had time to think about jungle rats and feel sorry for them. They were so hungry.

I left the jungle school feeling confident that escape, evasion and survival in heavy jungle was a good possibility. At least you didn't have to worry about freezing to death.

Chapter 4

In Country

During previous wars and all military and civil flying, my primary objective had always been survival. Heroic goals and macho images were not objectives in the past and I saw no reason to change. Based on previous experiences, several years of news media exposure and a lot of reading, I had formed an idea of what Vietnam would be like: little personal security and surprise attacks. My goal was to help the odds where possible by preparation. Never give the enemy a cheap shot. However, war does involve risks and I was prepared to take them. Just avoid unnecessary risks.

My first night was spent at the huge Bien Hoa Air Base and Army complex while awaiting a flight to Can Tho, Group Headquarters for all the Air Force FACs in Vietnam. Transient officers were put up in a group of steel Quonset huts with a single sand-bagged bunker in the center of the area. Before going to bed I walked the route to the bunker, just in case. Harry Longfellow was assigned to a bed in another hut, next to the bunker.

About 2:00 A.M. a series of 'whumps', loud bangs with echoes, woke me. I laid there a few seconds wondering, "Is that in-coming or out-going?" No one was moving in the hut. My first decision was that the bed was a stupid place to think about it. I should make that decision from inside the bunker. I was the first one in. Explosions continued, some close, some far. The bunker filled rather rapidly but no Harry. He was a deep sleeper. I stuck my head out of the doorway closest to him and yelled. No response. After several attempts, I ran over to his hut and yelled through the screen by his bed. I got a muffled reply. "Yeah, Brownie, what the hell is going on?" I explained to him the place was being attacked and he should be in the bunker. He was quiet for a minute. As it happened, there were no close bursts at that time. He said, "Sounds to me like it's almost over. I'll just stay here." I suppose he went right back to sleep.

More than one hundred 140 millimeter rockets hit the base that night. A few pieces of shrapnel or rocks made noisy landings on the metal Quonsets but no rocket hit within several hundred feet of us and I didn't feel threatened by the action.

A short flight the next morning to Can Tho, down on the Mekong delta, put me at Group Headquarters for some in-country check flights and receiving my duty assignment. The first night in Can Tho was like the night before at Bien Hoa – rockets and mortars hit the base about 2:00 A.M. Again, nothing close and I didn't feel threatened.

I was assigned to the 20th Tactical Air Support Squadron (TASS), based at Da Nang and given two jobs: Air Liaison Officer (ALO) for the First ARVN Division Commander headquarters in Hue, the very capable Brigadier General Ngo Quang Truong, plus supervising Air Force FAC detachments based in Hue and Quang Tri. The area between Da Nang and the DMZ was mine, all mine. Hot weather is not my bag so the farther north the better, and I had read about the beautiful city of Hue in *National Geographic*.

When I left Can Tho, Harry knew he was being assigned to some super-secret project but didn't know where he was going. As it turned out, six months later, he was working for me as chief of the Quang Tri FAC Detachment.

Da Nang was my next stop. There I met my boss and received another series of check-out flights. One night I had a chance to sit in the back seat and play with a 'star-light' scope. It was a fascinating device, a telescope with light amplification, where you could look out into blackness and see objects. They were displayed on a little screen in green. It had a small field of view so keeping an object under observation was difficult if the plane bumped or turned much. I gave up and watched the tracers and flashes around an outpost near Hoi An that was under attack.

Finally all the squares were filled, all the forms made out, all the briefings done, rules of engagement read and signed. The process took almost two weeks but now I could go to work.

National Geographic was right. Hue *was* a beautiful city – giant walls and moats reminded me of European castles. Some buildings were oriental in style; others looked like French villas. A clean, clear river, named Perfume, flowed gently past stately houses, an impressive walled fortress, delicate parks, marble steps, pagodas, lush trees and rounded grass banks. Tree-lined streets led to arched bridges over brick-lined moats and past heavy gates into royal residences and ornate state buildings. Nine huge brass cannons guarded the parade grounds. Our air strip was the former emperor's own, located inside the walled part of the city. I couldn't think of a more romantic, beautiful city yet I was there to wage war. A paradox.

A huge Catholic church in the southern part of the city had Vatican architectural roots but oriental-styled spires, an effective compromise. I wondered if the Vietnamese version of the Bible had similar compromises to fit far-eastern culture. To me, pounding an existing culture into someone else's mold was a waste. Perhaps Catholic values and stringent behavioral dictum had been rounded off some.

Two bridges crossed the Perfume. One, just a short block from the MACV compound, was primarily for vehicles and pedestrians. The other, near the western edge of the city, was built for the railroad that connected Hanoi and Saigon. Boards had been attached to the ties between the rails and out to their ends so vehicles could use it as well. Islands, canals and river channels lent themselves to boat traffic. Hue was a hub for commerce as well as a scenic place to live. A large open market area between the river and main street in the downtown area served both land and water traffic.

The Citadel, on the north bank, was an area surrounded by a wide, high wall, more or less square, with one face parallel to the Perfume River. The river, in front of the wall, ran southwest to northeast. Most city streets on the north side of the river were laid out in a rectangular grid parallel to the walls.

On the south side, street arrangement was more casual; some on a grid, some diagonals, some wandering.

First Division Headquarters (ARVN) was in a walled compound nestled in the north corner of the Citadel. The air strip was nearer the west corner. My home was the MACV compound across the river. It was a quarter of a block square, the outer perimeter defined in places by building sides, wire fences or masonry walls. Inside was a three-story hotel-like building with a two-story wing, a single residential style house at the back, a small chapel, a dispensary and three rows of brick and stucco hooches with sheet metal roofs. Total occupancy was about two hundred people, mostly U.S. Army.

Colonel Keeler (Army) was the senior advisor when I arrived. I liked him. He had a short muscular body, bald head, and was an outspoken, positive, direct person with what appeared to be a short temper. After he had laid my ears back a few times I saw the pattern. The only time he appeared to lose his temper was when someone did something that jeopardized himself or others. Keeler was a life saver.

When I arrived he was starting a push to increase compound security by building more bunkers, a guard tower on the vulnerable northeast corner, more concertina wire and machine gun emplacements. Every person was assigned a combat position for repelling an attack. Even though he had left the area months before, I thought of the good colonel many times during the Tet offensive and thanked him again and again. If physical defenses had not been improved over what they were when I arrived, the NVA would have been inside the compound within hours.

The Thua Thien Province Chief's compound was between ours and the Perfume River. It had a solid, high wall all the way around with only a few massive doors and appeared to be a very secure area.

My permanent room wasn't available when I arrived so I lucked into a VIP room in the residential style building located in the eastern corner. A high ceiling with a fan and big windows on two sides kept the room comfortable without air conditioning. I went to bed the first night wondering if the usual welcoming mortar attack would hit. Old hands told me the area was comparatively peaceful and there had been just two compound bombardments during the last year.

At that time there was only one bunker in the compound, by the gate. All buildings were made of solid, thick brick walls and columns covered with plaster to give a smooth finish. Bullets and shrapnel couldn't penetrate them. I pulled the bed about eighteen inches away from the wall so I could roll off and drop next to it if mortars came. Historically, the VC mortared, then attacked. I could get to a defensive position after the mortars stopped coming. Running around in shrapnel-filled air could be painful.

Nothing happened the first night. About two-thirty in the morning of the second night, the loudest noise I'd ever heard blasted me awake. These mortar shells were close and had instant fuses, intended for making casualties by bursting at ground level and scattering shrapnel. On our hard-packed gravel and cement grounds, they went off before penetrating the surface, no crater, so the sound wasn't muffled at all – like giant cherry bombs landing on a sidewalk.

My first motion was as planned – a quick roll out of the bed onto the floor. The rounds were coming in about every 20 or 30 seconds, long enough between them to think but not to do much. When the echoes of each explosion faded, I could hear people shouting. Were VC already in the compound? I had to look. I was right below a window. My M-16 was within reach. The routine was the same every time – flash (super brilliant white), crash (awesome eardrum-bursting concussion), tinkle (broken glass, either from concussion or shrapnel) – flash, crash, tinkle. Flash, crash, tinkle. I began taking short peeks out the window after the tinkles and before the flashes. Most of the yard lights were out. All I could see was dust and smoke, no movement.

I became aware of a new sound between the tinkles and the crashes. It was a barely audible, steady, high-pitched whine, similar to a siren I had on my bicycle thirty years before. "My God!" I thought. "Who the hell decided we needed a siren to let us know we were being attacked?" Maybe, somewhere, there was logic to support installing the little, pip-squeak thing but it seemed so stupid at the time. Bizarre.

They had our range, exactly. The 'wake-up' round hit in the west end of the compound and each successive shell was a little farther to the east. It wasn't hard to figure that out. Each crash was louder than the one before and the flashes coming through the windows kept getting brighter. They were like giant earth-shaking footsteps, each one a little closer.

One hit right in front of my room; glass from the windows and shrapnel were flying all around. I thought, "The next one will be right through the roof. They *are* trying to kill me." It didn't come. Neither did any ground attack. In military terms, the bombardment was probably meant to harass, convince us life would be better in the states. What it did do was motivate the troops to put higher priorities on building bunkers and other defenses.

After the echoes died down and I was reasonably sure there would be no more in-coming, I shook the glass and trash out of my shoes, put them on and crunched outside. Curiosity more than anything else got me moving since I hadn't been assigned to any defensive position. My ARVN Jeep, parked with its back up to the porch by my room, was a mess. The last round had hit about twenty feet in front of it. Water dribbled out of several holes in the radiator into a puddle that looked like blood in the dim light. Three tires were flat and the windshield broken. Colonel Keeler's staff car, parked next to my Jeep had been riddled too. The air conditioner in the Officers' Club, one week old, was also a casualty. Miraculously there were no serious wounds.

Next morning my ARVN driver became very upset when he saw the Jeep. I didn't understand why: you have to expect losses in war and a damaged Jeep should be no big deal. All he had to do was get their motor pool to put on three new tires and fix the radiator. Nothing happened for a week. I nagged. He knew a little English, just what he'd picked up from GIs, and I knew very little Vietnamese. One morning we stood in front of the wounded Jeep and tried to communicate. All I wanted to know was why couldn't it be fixed. The First Division Headquarters motor pool was right next to the airport and I had seen stacks of tires and mechanics working on vehicles every day. I could see he was working on an answer I might understand. When he had searched his inventory of English words and assembled a meaningful statement, he spoke: "Ah, sir, motor pool motherfucker; he full o' shit."

With that bit of information and some observations offered by MACV personnel, I concluded that the scratch system (bribes) of the far-east extended down to the lowest ARVN echelon. I couldn't stand the idea of paying cash to get their Jeep fixed. A bottle of whiskey, in lieu of cash, got the job done.

There were many things to learn about my new job, the men working for me, the area. It took about two weeks to understand *how* things were being done. *Whys* took a lot longer, with a few left forever only to my opinion.

Two FAC detachments were under my supervision, one in Hue and one in Quang Tri. Both averaged five to six pilots and three to five aircraft. Both had mechanics for aircraft maintenance and a small variety of specialists such as radio and armament technicians. Both had detachment commanders, usually majors, who scheduled missions and handled day-to-day matters for the detachment. The squadron headquarters in Da Nang supported them directly in administrative and supply matters. My responsibility was supervising their combat activities, to see that they were doing their jobs and getting the support they needed.

Each detachment commander had a second duty, being an Air Liaison Officer (ALO), working with the Province Chief and his regional forces (RF) plus ARVN combat units in the area. Work consisted of exchanging intelligence information, advising them on air support and working out operations plans.

The Quang Tri detachment lived in a small MACV compound built in a field on the edge of the city. Bunkers, berms, barbed wire and sand-bagged machine gun positions were the primary defenses. Most buildings were temporary types, made of wood, tin and canvas. They flew from a small gravel strip west of town. Air America, VNAF FACs and other air operations shared use of the strip.

Thua Thien detachment pilots and some of the mechanics lived in the MACV compound in Hue. My personnel (three or four radio operators) and the balance of the mechanics lived in a nice civilian-style residence, called House Eight, about two blocks away from the compound. I never learned who paid the rent on the house or why the arrangement had been made but the men who lived there liked it, despite the risks. Mama-Sans, dressed in attractive ao dais, came in daily to do the housework and washing. It had a low walled yard and many of the comforts of home. They had a machine gun, plenty of ammo and hand grenades besides their own M-16s for defense.

With squadron personnel down in Da Nang handling most administration (we didn't have a single clerk), the detachment commanders and I were free to do the things that should be done in combat areas. It was an excellent arrangement, further enhanced by the notion that Hue and Quang Tri were rather insecure areas, completely eliminating visits by squadron officials. They nagged us by telephone and radio and writing but no one from squadron or group ever came up to see what we were doing. It was wonderful.

Chapter 5

A Shau Valley

"Lead by example" is my favorite method for getting things done so I asked the Thua Thien detachment commander to schedule me for missions right along with his crew. The province had been divided into geographically defined areas and each assigned to one pilot for primary visual reconnaissance responsibility. The A Shau Valley and jungle area between it and Hue was unassigned when I arrived so it became my reconnaissance responsibility.

A Shau Valley had been in the news about nine months before then, when a pilot earned the Congressional Medal of Honor. A two-ship flight of the old work horses, propeller-driven A-1s were covering a hectic withdrawal of the last ARVN troops and U.S. advisors from the valley. The other plane's engine was damaged by enemy fire and the pilot had to make a forced landing on a runway near the abandoned outpost, even though one end of it was already held by enemy troops. He immediately landed too, taxied up to the disabled airplane, invited the downed pilot to sit on his lap, then turned around and took off through a hail of bullets.

I remembered the story as I circled that airstrip. New vegetation had covered the outpost, leaving only a green relief outline of berms. The runway had a few bomb craters in it but a fair portion appeared usable – more than enough for an O-1 to land. Would I dare do it too? They certainly wouldn't be expecting me. There was no observable activity in the whole valley except for road re-building. I dropped a little lower to see if any obstacles had been placed on the runway. It looked good – too good. What the hell was I thinking of? No cheap shots, remember? My ego would have to do without this stroke.

It was a beautiful valley, running northwest-southeast with rounded, jungle-covered mountains on both sides. The Laotian border ran along the west ridge, about twenty miles of rolling hilly jungle separated the eastern ridge from Hue. The south end was about fifty miles from Da Nang. It was a strategic valley. That was why the NVA took it and held it.

Mute evidence of the value we placed on the valley was all around. Hundreds of bomb craters, ten or fifteen helicopter and aircraft hulks littered the place. We called one ravine sloping up to the west ridge 'Helicopter Valley.' Four or five broken birds lay at odd angles within a quarter mile area. I wondered what happened there.

There was no doubt what the North Vietnamese were using the valley for – a highway to the heart of I Corps, the northern most quarter of South Vietnam. A good road had been built running east from the Ho Chi Minh trails in Laos up to the border. There it took a northern jog for about one-half a mile as it followed the top of a narrow saddle-back ridge into Vietnam, turned east again, going down along the open face of a rugged mountain into the A Shau Valley. From there it meandered to the south, tending towards the eastern side where a narrow road had been built years before. When I started my tour in Vietnam, the new, all-weather road had been completed to A Luoi, about one-third of the way down the valley. Six months later, the road disappeared into the jungle at the south end and a spur branched off at mid-point, going up over the west ridge directly toward Hue. It was about one-third complete. Road construction proceeded steadily despite my best efforts and countless air strikes.

I filed intelligence reports almost daily, hauled various ARVN officers and Col. Keeler out there to show them what was going on. It must have had some effect. We were allocated four air strikes a day for road interdiction – FACs picked the targets.

To me, it seemed the best place to break the road was where it ran along the face of the mountain. No simple detours around craters were possible. Bombs above the road would cause rock slides; bombs below would undermine the roadbed. The mountain face was composed entirely of loose rock, no vegetation or other cover was available.

Controlling air strikes in an area where there were no friendlies was a good opportunity to practice, so I selected target areas but did not put in more than my share of the strikes. Instead I sometimes accompanied other FACs (in another airplane) to point out targets and carry out my daily VR duties.

This is one of the P-40s used for preliminary fighter pilot training at Foster Field, near Victoria, Texas, in early 1944. Plenty of fresh air, no helmet and no "G" suit – the relaxed way to fly! Today's fighter pilots sit in pressurized compartments, wear heavy helmets and tight "G" suits.

This is a razor-back P-47 with a "paddle" prop, probably a D21 or D23 series. This photo was taken in November, 1944 at a B-29 base in India. We were on temporary duty there for a few weeks to defend the base from Japanese bomber attacks. They didn't come.

A 1954 Cessna 170-B. Many of them are still flying. I was so impressed with O-1 flying characteristics that I bought a 170-B (3253A) as soon as I returned from Vietnam. It was an excellent family airplane that carried four people. Cleaner lines than the O-1 gave it a higher cruising speed (115 MPH) despite its smaller (145 HP) engine. (Robert C. Mikesh)

An O-1F pictured at Holly Field, Florida in May 1967. Larger engine, narrow body and many more windows were the major differences between it and the 170-B. Wing racks for ordnance and many radios were added to support Forward Air Controller functions. The O-1F had a constant speed prop, a readily recognizable feature. (Robert C. Mikesh)

O-1s at Holley Field await the day's activity in training fighter pilots to be Forward Air Controllers. Some proved to be exciting –pilots experienced in only jet fighters with tricycle landing gears often found taking off and landing slow planes, with the third wheel in back, required some skills they didn't have at first. (Robert C. Mikesh)

Bunker covering the gate to the MACV compound. The mortar tube behind the barrel was one used by VC during an earlier attack on the compound. It was captured by ARVN troops.

Dates on the mortar silhouettes reminded us of some of the first compound bombardments. After a while, no one bothered to keep the sign up to date. I arrived May 14, just in time. (Robert C. Mikesh)

This highly treasured air conditioner in the "Officers' Club" (a one-room bar) was destroyed by VC mortar shrapnel less than a week after being installed.

VIP quarters in the Hue MACV compound. Shortly after this photo was taken, a guard tower was erected at the compound corner immediately to the left of the building.

Parking lot for the MACV compound in Hue. The canteen and gun belt with M-16 and map case indicate I'm on my way to the airport and a flight. My room was to the extreme left of the photo, on the second floor. The dining room, theater and other facilities were in the building behind me. (Robert C. Mikesh)

First ARVN Division headquarters. The Air Force communications center for FACs was on the second floor. Eleven antennae are on the roof.

Col. Keeler's staff car after a mortar attack on the Hue MACV compound, May, 1967. Plenty of fresh air in the body but no air in the tires.

Above: *An O-1E flying over Thua Thien Province in the northern part of South Vietnam. This particular airplane (500) became my favorite. We spent many hours together over A Shau Valley and it always got me back to friendlier territory. (Robert C. Mikesh)*

Right: A "mortar motel" similar to the one I used in Bien Hoa. Not much for comfort but great for security when it's raining rocket and mortar shells. Speeds of personnel moving from their adjacent "hooches" to the bunkers varied between "stop-and-watch" to super-sonic, depending on personalities and shell proximities. (Robert C. Mikesh)

A C-123 delivering fuel for FAC aircraft at Hue had to be backed into a corner to clear the runway. Fuel was carried in a large rubber bladder that laid on the cargo compartment floor. It took courage and skill to deliver gasoline to Hue. We appreciated their help. (Robert C. Mikesh)

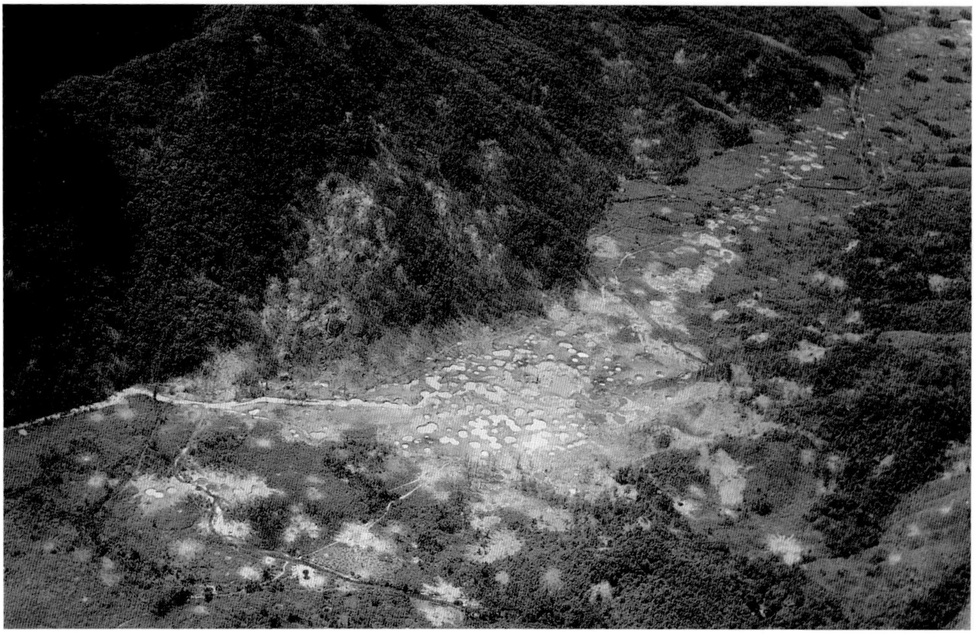

A good example of a choke point on the NVA-constructed road in A Shau valley. The road descended into the valley from the upper right corner of this photo. Steep hills on both sides and a stream narrowed possible courses at this point. Facs directed air strikes into the choke area, completely destroying the road many times. Yet, on mornings after, there would be fresh tire tracks as evidence that trucks had gone through. Old (6 months) B-52 strike is visible as a partially over-grown string of craters angled off to the upper right. Many B-52 strikes were based on FAC reports. (Robert C. Mikesh)

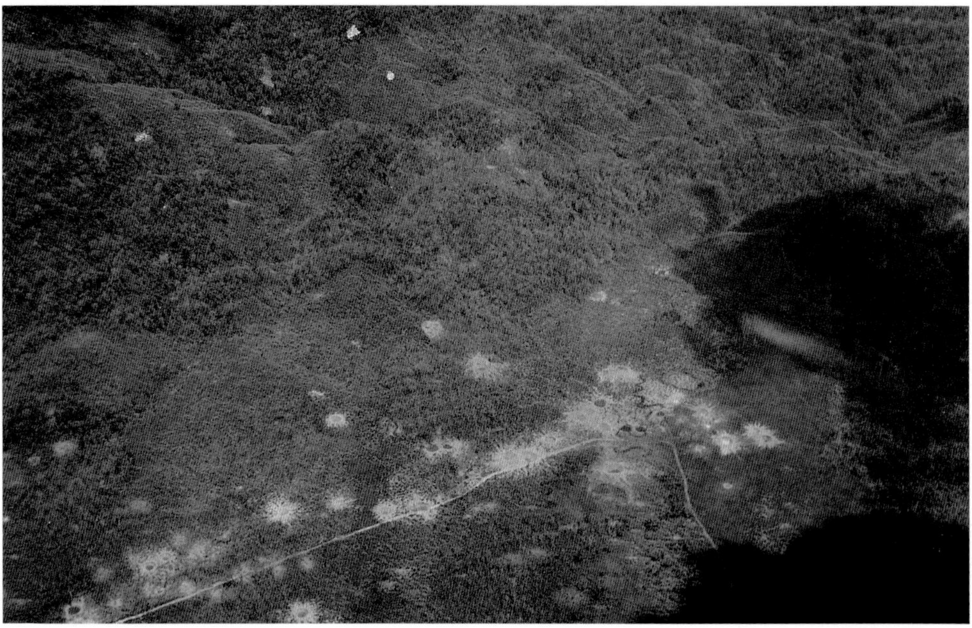

Another choke point. There was a bridge across a stream where the road makes a 90 degree turn. The road then descended along the side of a hill (lower left) so some bombs were directed on it after the bridge was taken out. (Robert C. Mikesh)

Airstrip along the side of a Laotian village. FACs landed here occasionally to bring in school supplies and medicine. A few days after this photo was taken, the NVA destroyed the village in maneuvers relative to the Tet offensive.

"Elephant" outpost in Laos. It was located between NVA forces guarding the Ho Chi Minh trails and the Vietnam border near Khe Sanh.

This scene in the Citadel residential area of Hue after Tet testifies to the violence of the battle.

Helicopters at the Hue airport destroyed by NVA satchel charges during the battle.

Military tires are tough. I discovered this rifle bullet protruding from a tire on my Jeep after a trip to the airport. Since it wasn't leaking, I left it there.

Erosion by bullets, shrapnel and concussion peeled the stucco facing off the Post Office building, revealing its brick structure.

This O-1 was the sole survivor of the battle. The wings were removed in preparation for helicopter airlift to Da Nang. However they were stolen during the night so only the fuselage and tail made it back.

A nice home used to stand behind the steps. A small bomb or large artillery shell leveled it. Part of the Citadel wall is visible in the background.

O-2 pieces and two of the CONEX boxes we used to store munitions and supplies. War is messy.

A school building near the Hue airport – mute evidence of building-by-building, room-by-room fighting.

O-1 and helicopter remains. The sand-bagged bunker behind the O-1 was in an ARVN motor pool. It appeared to have been over-run during the battle.

The battle was definitely hard on houses. People were living in this pile of rubble, under a few boards and a piece of sheet metal.

A dud anti-tank round damaged the door frame on the extreme right. The smoking hot shell landed on a bed, beside one of the room's occupants.

Bunker and trench made by NVA on top of the Citadel wall near the Cau Huu gate.

NVA trenches dug into the top of the Citadel wall. That's the Cua Thuong Tu gate tower in the background.

One of the University buildings gutted by fire. The bodies of three German doctors, in Vietnam as volunteers to teach, were found near here. They had been killed by bullets through their heads.

The north end of the railroad bridge was dropped by NVA sappers. A ramp bulldozed down to the end made it usable.

It was a good airplane. Note the damaged wall and bent CONEX's. The airport was the scene of several intense battles.

Three O-1s destroyed by satchel charges. The fourth escaped serious damage.

Residential area of Hue, inside the Citadel walls.

Runway and ramp at the Hue airport, post-battle. That's Sgt. Dong, the airport manager. He and his family lived at the airport. His boss, Lt. Koung, died in a fox-hole at the end of the runway.

Downtown Hue is to the left. The main bridge across the Perfume River is to the right. The tank, probably an M-48, was destroyed during the battle.

Duong Dinh Bo Linh Street, between the downtown area and the 1st ARVN Division headquarters, after the battle.

The street leading from downtown Hue to the Cua Thuong Tu gate.

My 'short round' investigation armada. Nearest to the camera is Tom Young. Next is a Vietnam Army interpreter assigned to duty in Laos. Two Laotian army guards are in the accompanying 'gun-boat.'

Laotian houses were very functional, comfortable dwellings. They offered reasonably dry, cool interiors in a typically hot, humid environment.

A "friendly fire" bomb crater in Laos. No damage here except to re-shape Mother Earth. We made a lot of "matchsticks" and waterholes out in the jungle.

Laotian house destroyed by "friendly fire" – U.S. Air Force pilots about 100 miles from their directed area of patrol. The bomb landed in a nearby creek. It appeared the weight of the mud falling on its roof caused it to topple. I apologized to the man who was inside it when the bomb hit. The interpreter said the man's hearing was still very bad. No wonder!

B-52s start a load of bombs towards their final destination. At typical bombing altitude B-52s couldn't be seen or heard by people on the ground. No warning at all, tremendous concussion, shock waves, tons of debris, shattering violence, terror . . . No fun. (USAF via Robert C. Mikesh)

The fighter/bomber pilots were good; F-100s were usually the most accurate. Every day, weather permitting, they'd take out a portion of the road, sometimes a couple of hundred feet. Next morning, what do you know, the road would be whole again. The NVA must have had hundreds of workers and good equipment to repair the road and get trucks over it in one night. I hoped the constant bombing would cause a giant rock-slide and take out a major section but it didn't happen.

Capt. Bud Fletcher found they were getting upset about our anti-road campaign. During the second week into the program, Bud was working on the cliff face with a brace of fighters when the sky became filled with 'orange golf balls.' That's what 50-caliber tracer bullets look like – orange golf balls going like mad. One came through the side of his plane, cut the laces on his boot and tore his sock but didn't scratch him.

Those so-and-so's on the ground had moved a quad-fifty (that's four 50-caliber machine guns on one mount) up near the top of the mountain. At least, that's what we thought it was, based on the hail of bullets it put out. We tried to destroy the thing but were handicapped by the fact that when you got low enough to see it, you are low enough to get shot. Also, they kept moving it around.

Down on the valley floor, the road crossed a deep gully on a wooden bridge about fifty feet long. Again, there was no easy detour so that became my new target. They could keep their quad-fifty up on the mountain.

With four strikes (that's eight fighters) a day, all hauling bombs, usually 500-pounders, plus a few 750s, the area around that bridge soon looked like a major disaster. Every day, weather permitting, the bridge was damaged or destroyed. Every night, it was repaired or rebuilt. Yet, in hundreds of hours of flying over A Shau, I never saw a human or evidence of recent habitation anywhere in the valley. I did locate a few truck parks and bulldozer tracks, but I never saw a human move.

Where did they come from to repair and build the road? Where did they go? Where were they during the day? It couldn't be that I was not looking, couldn't see, because I did spot people on or near the road east and west of the valley. Maybe they left the valley every morning. Here was a big green valley with 'abandoned' airfields, villages, fortresses and farms, a good road being built and rebuilt along its length but absolutely no visible evidence of anyone living there. I tried many things to catch them in the open. Several times, when the weather was right, I'd climb to twelve thousand feet over the coast, throttle back to a little above idle when starting over the jungle and glide all the way into the A Shau. Sometimes I'd drop in through clouds, sometimes try to sneak in at dawn, or at last light, or even at night, but never saw a thing move in the valley. I concluded they had excellent aircraft spotter and communication systems, perhaps even radar.

After about two weeks of bombing on that bridge, they build a new road down to a wide shallow stream a half mile west of the bridge and drove down it until well past the gully, then back to the road. I could see truck tracks under the water.

Without the bridge as a choke-point, our only choices were reduced to visual clues. For example, we'd hit stands of tall trees near the road if there were any tracks leading off the road towards the trees. Sometimes it worked. We knew something was hit when the bombs triggered secondary explosions or petroleum-based fires (lots of black smoke). Occasionally FACs carried mixed loads of HE (high explosive) and WP rockets, firing HE rockets into suspicious areas to see what developed. Also, during hot, dry periods, we started grass and brush fires. Oddly, HE rockets worked better than WP for lighting them.

After Tet, the U.S. Army began setting up artillery fire bases west of Hue. One of them had some long range guns that could reach into A Shau Valley. Now I could set up H & I (harassment and interdiction) fire missions. I'd go out to the valley during the day and adjust fire by having them fire test rounds at certain parts of the road. At night, the army would fire rounds towards aim points at random times which, if they didn't hit any trucks, at least made the drivers nervous.

One day I selected a short wooden bridge as the aim point. To my amazement, the second or third round of adjusting fire went right through the bridge – at a twenty-mile range that's damned good or very lucky. Since the bridge was badly damaged, my first impulse was to select a new aim point, but then I thought, "No, someone will have to fix it." I told the fire base to really work it over that night. Next morning the bridge had been repaired, there were craters all around the bridge and fresh tire tracks on the road where explosions had thrown a coating of dirt.

I appreciated not being on that repair crew. It must have been exciting.

Daily bombing, directed by FACs, continued for several months; so did the road. During my tour, the war in A Shau was strictly between FACs and NVA. Some LRRPs (long range reconnaissance patrols) were put in along the eastern ridge but only FAC-directed air strikes and long range guns adjusted by FACs provided any deterrent to the enemy.

The army advised us when LRRPs were in the jungle and about where they were. We'd monitor designated radio frequencies while over the jungle so they could contact us if they needed help. FACs came in handy for relaying messages when patrols were out of radio range with their base. One time, as I was flying over the last ridge into the valley, I heard a whisper in my earphones. With all my radios on, I couldn't be sure which one was receiving it and I wasn't sure what was said. I waited. After a short time, the whisper started again and I picked out enough words to realize someone was asking an unidentified FAC overhead to give him a call. I turned up the volume on my FM radio, LRRP frequency, and asked the caller to speak louder. I could hear better with the volume up but he was still whispering. First he apologized for whispering, explaining there were a bunch of NVA troops within two hundred feet and then requested a withdrawal later that day, giving me coordinates (encoded) for a pick-up. He was one cool cat. That's probably why he led the LRRP. I carried the message back to the army rather than use one of my transmitters because of the probability someone in the NVA or VC had captured (or bought) a code book. Because of altitude, aircraft radios can be heard over much greater distances than ground stations, thus increasing the possibility that NVA or VC personnel with access to codes could intercept a message.

Late one afternoon, I was VRing the north end of A Shau while monitoring the radios on an LRRP extraction, Jim Jones, one of my FACs, had been sent out to assist. The squad was located in an area of low ridges between the south end of the valley and Hue. It turned nasty. The NVA had discovered their presence and hoards of troops were doing their best to kill them before they could be extracted. Trying to get the helicopters and the friendlies to a suitable pick-up point at the same time was proving difficult. Also, Jim was trying to protect them by putting in air strikes, not an easy task when both friends and enemy are in motion. I decided he might need help and headed south. By the time I got there, another factor complicated the project – Jones was running out of gas. I'd been up for about an hour and a half so I was good for another hour. Jim helped me find the friendlies, then headed for Hue. I put in two flights of fighters, one on the ridge ahead of them to move out any VC and clear an LZ, and one behind them to slow down the pursuers. The sun dipped below the horizon as the last few fighter passes were made. I called for a flare-ship; this was going to be a night extraction. About then, the helicopters had to leave for more fuel. Things were going to hell in the air as well as on the ground. There was a lot of small caliber shooting at the aircraft, but no anti-aircraft guns.

It was too early in the evening; no flare-ships were airborne. Two fresh helicopters showed up and the troops said they were on the ridge, so I started a blacked out pick-up. First I had to find exactly where the troops were. It was dark now and I was down to about fifteen minutes of fuel. I asked for a position light. Within one minute, there were about ten lights showing. They obviously had radios and people who understood English. The sergeant, fortunately, was the only one with a hooded strobe light.

I was facing a fifteen-minute flight to Hue with possibly less than fifteen minutes of fuel. Jim arrived back on the scene so I headed for home at slow speed to save fuel while he successfully completed the extraction. Next morning Sgt. Shanklin, our aircraft maintenance chief, said both my tanks were absolutely empty.

The road from Ho Chi Minh trails in central Laos climbed the south side of a long valley as it approached the border. There were a lot of poorly concealed tracks off the road and into tree covered areas within the last one thousand feet before it made a sharp left turn and crossed the unmarked border into Vietnam. Those tracks defined well-used truck parks, protected by Washington's rules of engagement (Laos was 'off limits') as they were prescribed to me. Then it followed the top of a narrow ridge, passing through a clump of trees about halfway across. Other than those trees, the only vegetation on the ridge was low bushes and short grass. I circled that ridge the day Col. Keeler rode out with me. As I crossed the road I could see down it into the wooded area. Much to my surprise, there was a group of people standing in the road. They must have thought I wouldn't be able to see them. I turned and asked Col. Keeler, "Did you see those guys standing there looking at us?" The intercom wasn't working so he just nodded. I asked him if he'd mind my taking the time to put a few air strikes on them. He didn't.

The Direct Air Support Center (DASC) loved live targets so I got a couple of flights approved quickly, although it would take a while to get them out there.

I continued to circle the trees. They couldn't walk out; not enough cover. After about fifteen minutes, I saw a few crawling in the grass by the side of the road. I fired a rocket, hitting the road right next to them. They were back in the trees within seconds.

Now that there was no doubt in their minds that they had been spotted, everyone started shooting at us. I had heard shots from the ground many times before and could readily separate them from other sounds common to an O-1 flying with the windows open but I wasn't sure if Col. Keeler knew. I turned around and said, "They're shooting at us," but the words were needless. One look at his face told me he knew.

My fuel situation was getting tight. Col. Keeler was no lightweight and that increased fuel consumption. It was a long way back to Hue. I asked for another FAC to come out and take over if I had to leave before the air got there.

Finally, two flights arrived and we went to work. I'd fired another rocket to keep them pinned down so there were only two left for target marking. I wanted planes with napalm and twenty millimeter cannons. The first flight had only bombs and they didn't hit the trees. Bud Fletcher got there about the same time as the second flight so I headed for the barn. I'd been flying two hours and twenty minutes, five more than I normally considered 'bingo' time in the A Shau area and had extra distance to cover with a heavier load. Using all the energy conservation rules, I set up a slow descent that would put me at sea level, the altitude at Hue, in about twenty-five minutes, and throttled back to best L/D (lift over drag) speed. We made it to the runway but the engine quit, out of gas, before I could park it. Col. Keeler's normally neat, starched khakis were rumpled and sweaty. I didn't ask and he never suggested another flight with me.

Next morning I checked the clump of trees. There weren't any. A few more names of little people who meant nothing to big people were probably added to the roster of those heroes who sacrificed their lives so that South Vietnam could be freed from the imperialistic invaders – us. At least that's what the North Vietnam government was telling its people.

I tried to get Gen. Truong to ride out with me and view the road progress in A Shau but he elected to go in a Huey with Col. Keeler and my roommate, Maj. Domenicucci. They got too curious and too low. NVA opened up on them with the General getting a bullet through his hat and many holes in the helicopter.

The O-l was appreciated by its pilots but it wasn't big, wasn't jet-powered and certainly not elegant. Too bad. It was a sweet flying, very functional machine.

The road being built towards Hue bothered me the most, probably because that was where I lived. It was wider and appeared used more and better made than the branch going south towards Da Nang. I spent many hours over the area between A Shau and Hue looking for whatever was being brought in over the road. The land was generally rolling hills covered by dense growth. Small streams wound through the area. During my first months in country, I could see Montagnards working their hillside farms in this area, using the tropical slash and burn technique, and their homes, built out of poles and leaves. Sometimes I circled them and waved. They didn't wave back but they didn't shoot at me either. Suddenly, in a matter of weeks, all farming stopped and the Montagnards disappeared. Later I heard the NVA conscripted them as slave labor on their roads.

In September, I began finding new foot bridges and paths in the jungle area five to ten miles west of Hue. I filed more intelligence reports and hauled more ARVN observers out to see both the roads and trails. Finally, a few B-52 strikes were put into areas where most activity was evident.

The strikes were comforting in one respect: the enemy was catching hell and I wasn't. In another way they were discomforting: the NVA was getting closer. Since they were in my VR area, I usually did the BDAs (bomb damage assessments). It was hard to find any evidence of personnel killed or material destroyed in jungle areas. Those seven hundred and fifty pound bombs made huge holes, either blowing things into the jungle or burying them. Watching a strike was an experience in violence, tremendous flashes with gray/white shock waves radiating out for hundreds of feet, debris being thrown about a hundred feet up and out around each crater.

I liked to do BDAs about fifteen minutes after a B-52 strike; time for the dust to settle but, hopefully, the survivors still in a state of shock so I could get down low without risking too much. Sometimes I'd find footprints that meandered over the freshly turned earth or suspicious objects but never saw a positively identifiable body.

One BDA was interesting. The strike was just on the other side of the first ridge west of Hue. I could hear it going in right on schedule as I climbed into the O-1. A young ARVN intelligence lieutenant, a pleasant person who spoke a little English, was going with me. We planned to head out to A Shau after doing the BDA.

Fifteen minutes later we were flying right down the middle of the strike zone. My altitude was around seven hundred feet. Both of us were looking down, intent on finding some evidence of enemy destruction, when suddenly it seemed like the whole earth exploded. Shock waves shook the plane, eardrum-shattering noise, wham, bam violence. I made an instant turn to the left, surprised that the wings were still on. I knew what had happened by then – one B-52 was a little late.

I circled outside the strike zone for about five minutes, waiting for the dust and my pulse rate to settle. What amazed me was how the bombs missed us. We had been right in the middle of the area they hit. Maybe that's another advantage for the O-l: they are small.

I started back towards the strike zone to finish the BDA. A scream came out of the back seat, as if someone had been stabbed. One look at the lieutenant's face told me I'd have to go back to the field and drop him off before finishing the BDA. I think he decided to pursue another career field; I never saw him again.

My reports, plus many others I'm sure, convinced Gen. Truong that the jungle area between A Shau and Hue could be rich in supply caches, NVA and VC. A search and destroy type of sweep was set up. Our army supported it by air-lifting most of the ARVN troops into a grassy valley eight miles back in the hills. The plan was for the troops to walk back to Highway One where they would be picked up and brought back to Hue. That's what they did. A few small caches found and a few light enemy contacts, that's all the sweep accomplished.

There were so many VC sympathizers within ARVN ranks at all levels that surprise was impossible on large operations such as that one. Also, I believe there was a tacit understanding between the troops involved: "We won't look hard; you don't shoot much."

The A Shau Valley was re-occupied briefly and at a high cost in lives by U.S. and ARVN forces during late April and early May 1968, after I had rotated. Traffic resumed, I'm sure, shortly after their departure. All in all, A Shau Valley was a successful endeavor for the NVA. They drove the ARVN troops and American advisors out, held and used the valley for many years despite our best efforts. Yet, back home, our families were being told we were winning the war. As I said many times in my correspondence, "not where I am."

Chapter 6

SHORT ROUNDS

The classic application of artillery for centuries involved a battle-line of soldiers with artillery pieces located somewhere behind them. Shells were fired over the friendlies to, hopefully, land on the enemy. If the gunners were off for some reason (too little powder, gun elevation too low) and the round (shell) fell short, it could hurt the wrong people. Long rounds weren't too bad; they were the enemy's problem.

The term 'short round' has been extended in modern warfare to cover any form of ordnance expended that harms friendlies. Someone decided I would be responsible for investigating all short round incidents involving the Air Force and occurring between Da Nang and the DMZ. There were only two incidents serious enough for me to make formal investigations and prepare reports so the additional duty didn't create much work. Risk, yes; but work, no. Both were interesting cases that led me to places I hadn't been before.

The first one involved a Marine platoon in a night defensive position near the DMZ. They were under attack by a much larger force of NVA and their situation was desperate. For some reason, effective artillery support wasn't available so a Spooky from Da Nang was sent up to help. Although the weather was good, no Marine FAC was available and my Quang Tri FACs weren't advised of the situation.

Spooky set up his radios so he could talk directly with the platoon leader. The pilot could see ground fire but there was simply wasn't any way to positively identify the friendlies. In desperation the leader accepted less than positive identification of their position and cleared Spooky to begin firing. The pilot put the plane in a tight circle with its center about where he thought the NVA were and turned on his side shooting high speed Gatling guns. Lead rained down on the area, wounding a substantial portion of the Marines as well as the NVA.

Next morning my phone rang. I was directed to get the facts and make a report as soon as possible. A few phone calls later, I knew the wounded, including the platoon leader, had been medevac-ed to a Navy hospital ship in the Gulf of Tonkin and I could get a helicopter ride out to the ship from the airfield at Dong Ha.

I stuck a scratch pad into my map case and headed for the airport. At Dong Ha I parked the O-1 on pierced-steel planking near the Marine helicopter operations area and started looking for a ride. In minutes I was on my way out to the ship. I began to have a little apprehension about my reception in a Navy sickbay full of Marines shot up by the Air Force. Inter-service rivalry existed and, when one service goofed up, others tended to rub salt into the wound. I wasn't concerned about a physical confrontation but I expected uncooperative, truculent witnesses with a goal of revenge for their pain and suffering.

Seas were heavy and the landing deck was going up and down like a yo-yo. It was obvious the pilot had done this sort of thing many times before. He put the helicopter into hover and waited for the right time, then set it down as softly as anyone could reasonably expect. The gusty winds and heaving deck made me stagger like a drunk as I made my way to the hatch.

Minutes later I was ushered into a sick-bay that held several of the men I wanted to talk to. It didn't look at all like a hospital; double bunks in close quarters with dim lights. As I introduced myself and began asking questions, more men wandered in and sat down or leaned against the bunks to steady themselves as the ship rocked. All had been wounded by Spooky. I was pleased to see that none of them appeared to be seriously hurt. I asked if any had died or were critical. They looked at each other and discussed the condition of a few that weren't there, then came to the conclusion that none were critical and no one had died.

Their attitude was cooperative and forgiving. No hostility was shown. When I started to apologize for the error, several interrupted with comments like, "Man, it's no big deal; forget it; they were doing the best they could. We were better off with Spooky than we would have been without him."

I don't remember how many were wounded; somewhere between ten and twenty. A question kept coming up in my mind: With so many wounded, why weren't any critical or dead? Normal distribution of combat casualties would have several dead and several critical. I inquired about the types of wounds. Most had flesh wounds, slugs embedded in their buttocks, legs and arms. It was obvious they had been wearing their flak jackets and helmets. It was also obvious that Spooky had been too high and the bullets had lost most of their energy before getting down to the ground. That was fortunate in this case. NVA troops, without flak jackets, probably had worse wounds.

I didn't learn anything that could have been useful in avoiding that short round or preventing another under similar circumstances. A FAC familiar with the area might have helped. I couldn't find out why one hadn't been requested, other than no one thought about it. My recommendation was going to be short and simple: when in doubt, call your local FAC. I shook hands with the troops, complimented them on their objective outlook and left, with an inward sigh of relief.

The pilot on the helicopter warned me that NVA artillery shells (from across the DMZ) had been hitting the air base at Dong Ha frequently the last two hours and he wouldn't be on the ground very long. I jumped out as soon as the wheels hit. He was gone in seconds and I was alone, very much alone, out there in the middle of that big, flat, cover-less ramp. Everyone else was in bunkers. My O-1 appeared intact, about five hundred feet west. Bunkers and a measure of security, for the moment, were about two hundred and fifty feet north. It was decision time. I took the direct route to my airplane, based on less total distance traveled. True, if shelling stopped before I *had* to go to the airplane, I'd have reduced exposure, but it was getting late in the day and I'd really rather be some place else.

There were no craters or torn-up steel planking near the O-1 so I dispensed with the usual walk-around check. As soon as the engine was running, I called the tower for take-off instructions and, out of habit, started a quick engine check. Just as I switched to one magneto, the plane shuddered and there was a loud bang, like a backfire, typical when one magneto has gone bad. I thought, "Damn. What a time for engine problems." However, the tachometer did not indicate an excessive RPM drop. I completed the check, looked up from the instrument panel to start my taxi and then I saw what had made the bang. About seventy-five or one hundred feet directly ahead of me, the steel planking was all torn up and there was a good-sized crater right in the middle of the mess. It wasn't there when I got in the airplane. It was time to leave and I did. Fortunately, there was no other aircraft traffic.

My phone rang early on the morning of January 28. It was the Squadron Operations officer in Da Nang. He said there had been a short round up north; he couldn't say where, but I was to fly up to Khe Sanh immediately and contact a certain Air Force captain. I would have to learn more about the incident from him. I pressed for a little more information. He sounded confused or very badly informed. The best estimate he would give me was some fighters possibly strafed Lang Vei, a Special Forces manned outpost about three miles west of Khe Sanh. I asked if he was sure a short round had occurred. Khe Sanh was hot then, being supplied by air drops, and just getting on the ground in one piece was a challenge. I'd hate to risk my life on a wild goose chase. He said the only place I could get more information was at Khe Sanh so that was where I went.

From the air, Khe Sanh looked like a king-sized ant hill that a giant with size 100 waffle-stomper shoes had tried to kick to pieces. Bunkers, zig-zag trenches, piles of rubble and broken things like airplanes, helicopters, half-tracks, trucks and dismembered buildings littered the irregular surface of loose, freshly turned earth. The 'tower' recommended I keep my pattern in close and expect ground fire. I held my altitude at three thousand feet until directly over the field, then dumped full flaps, throttled back to idle, stuck the nose down to maximum speed for the flap setting and came down in a corkscrew shaped pattern instead of the usual rectangle.

I parked in the small ramp area north of the runway. There were no other planes on the ground. I knew why. Planes were 'mortar magnets.' Their presence attracted a rash of mortar and artillery shells. A jeep pulled up alongside as soon as my engine stopped and an Air Force pilot walked up to the plane. Capt. Tom Young told me the short round had occurred in Laos. A pair of roving Air Force fighters had strafed and bombed some friendly villages. There was an abandoned airstrip a few miles from the villages. The runway was still usable. Since he knew the airstrip and area, he suggested it would be better if he flew the plane.

As I was getting settled in back, he pointed out a problem. I had a large camera kit (a Pentax with various lenses, Air Force issue for FACs to photograph BDAs, etc.), my M-16 with extra ammo magazines, my Colt 45 in a holster and a note pad. He asked if I wanted to carry my M-16 all day, along with all the other stuff, and suggested I could leave it in a near-by CONEX container. Tom ran over to it and set my gun and magazines inside.

Shells were coming in often and getting close so we decided to take off and he'd fill me in a little better while flying to the airstrip. It seemed that fighters were sometimes given road interdiction missions. Their instructions, typically, were to cruise along the Ho Chi Minh Trails (several more or less parallel roads) in an area of Laos and shoot up anything that looked like a truck and any buildings within a certain distance (I think it was one thousand feet) of the roads. They were to assume that any structures close to roads had some highway support function and destroy them. The big mystery was why these particular villages were attacked. They were twenty miles east of the nearest known NVA-held position, about one hundred miles from the area where fighters were cleared for roving destruction missions and one to two miles from the nearest road.

Tom said the Laotian troops in this area were supported by both South Vietnam and U.S. (C.I.A.) and that they had been effective in preventing eastward movement of NVA forces towards the Vietnam border, Lang Vei and Khe Sanh.

Just a few miles into Laos, we descended towards an outpost on the north side of a valley. Tom tried the radio. The outpost's call sign was 'Elephant.' Nothing was moving when we arrived but, as we circled, a few people started walking around inside the fortified area. After a little delay, Elephant answered in fairly good English and Tom asked the man to meet him at the strip. We circled a little longer as a few men gathered around a small army truck, climbed in and started out the gate.

We landed on the rough grass strip and taxied up to a village that touched one side of it. By the time we got out of the O-1, there were about twenty people, adults and children, standing at a low bamboo fence, about eighteen inches high, that marked the boundary between the village and the strip. They were friendly; smiling and giving polite little waves when recognized. I was amazed how well-behaved the children were in contrast to the Vietnamese. No shouting, no shoving, no begging. Two older men who appeared to have authority arrived and we walked towards them; more smiles and bows but no understandable words. Tom explained to me that he and other FACs had been bringing school supplies and medicine (primarily highly desired aspirin) to the village for a while and the villagers appreciated their gifts.

About this time, the topless army truck arrived in a cloud of dust. Besides the driver, it contained a Laotian captain, an ARVN lieutenant and several soldiers.

Both officers knew Tom and greeted him warmly. The captain did not speak English but the Vietnamese lieutenant spoke both Laotian and English. Sometimes we had problems understanding his English and sometimes the captain had problems understanding his Laotian but with smiles, patience and some sign language supplements, we communicated.

The captain was a very confident-appearing extrovert who spoke in a loud voice and laughed a lot. I wondered how he maintained a positive attitude and managed to survive with such a small combat unit out here so close to major NVA forces. Perhaps it was the FACs and the air power they could apply that kept the NVA away. From all appearances, the Laotians thought Tom could walk on water.

I asked about the villages attacked by our planes. So far as the captain knew, no one had been killed or seriously wounded and there had been no major damage. I asked if it would be possible to visit the villages. I wanted to apologize to the village chiefs for the terrible mistake, assure them of our friendship, assess the damages and make arrangements for restitution. The captain said it could be arranged, gave several orders and his men scattered as we were led into the village.

An older man with white hair and a short beard said something to the interpreter and he asked if we would mind a short tour through the village, that the chief would like to show us around. I was pleased to get the invitation. Learning how people adjust to their environment has always been interesting to me. In such a primitive place, what mental and physical solutions had they used to create the quiet, reasonably comfortable life style I perceived from looking at the village?

First we were taken through the school. It was the largest building in the village and appeared big enough to serve several communities the size of the one we were in.

Next we headed for the only building with a metal roof. The rest were covered with thatch. It was pyramid shaped with hand h e w n wood frame. Board walls were arranged to allow good ventilation. In the middle was an assembly of boards that looked like a chimney but a few wood figures at the base and joss sticks showed me it was a Buddhist shrine. The building was a temple.

It wasn't much compared to the giant glossy temples and pagodas I'd seen in China and Japan but, with what they had in that little village, it was a significant structure. The old man waited as I looked around then pointed, with a smile, to the roof. A large object was suspended directly above me. It was a giant model of an 0-1. The wing span was about twelve feet, it had details such as landing gear, propeller, wing struts, tail wheel and even the rocket tubes. The frame was made of bamboo, then covered with magazine pages laboriously glued together. The interpreter said it was a symbol of appreciation for all the good things that had come to the village in O-1s.

We moved towards a river behind the village. There were two dug-out canoes and several natives with paddles waiting for us. The water was so clear I could see every stone on the bottom. How do you get into a dug-out canoe? One person at a time and very carefully.

It was like squatting on a tight rope. There were no seats and the thing had no stability. All four passengers, the Laotian captain, the ARVN lieutenant, Capt. Young and I tried to move as little as possible so the boatmen could do the balancing. There were a few times I thought we'd all get a chance to swim in the inviting water but we arrived at another village about one mile up-stream still reasonably dry.

We visited two villages, took photos of bomb and rocket craters, interviewed village chiefs and made notes on the damages (fortunately all were minor), apologized to all concerned and assured them the United States would make full restitution as soon as possible.

On the way back, I thought about the people I'd met and found many reasons to envy them. It was late January and the weather was warm and dry, the river was clean and clear, the children well behaved, their homes simple but comfortable, the pace was slow and they laughed a lot, pressures common to urban life were non-existent. It was true, their standard of living was low, almost aboriginal, but they didn't have the things we have too much of: pollution, pressure and taxes. I thought some day I'd like to return and try living their way for a few months. Maybe I'd learn something.

I said good-bye to the delegation at the landing strip, assuring them that I, or my representative, would return as soon as possible with some form of compensation. I didn't know what form it would be; money wouldn't do them any good. Food, clothing, school and medical supplies would be appreciated. I'd have to see what could be done.

Tom flew back to Khe Sanh. He taxied to the little ramp so I could change seats and pick up my M-16. The CONEX was gone. Instead there was a good-sized shell crater and bits of torn metal where it had been. There was no point in even looking for my gun. I thanked Tom, got in the front seat and left.

That's one thing I like about war. For the most part, accountability ceases. In peacetime you have to sign receipts for anything the government lets you use. I've been required to sign on the dotted line for a two-dollar plotter and, when I lost it, pay for another. In wartime, I could lose an M-16, get eight airplanes assigned to me destroyed, have my radio jeep annihilated and no one ever said a word.

Next morning, I flew down to Da Nang, interviewed the fighter pilots, wrote out my report, turned in the film and headed back to Hue. I planned to arrange for compensation after Tet. Things were tense in my provinces and I felt much more useful up there. The cause for the short round was simple; the pilots were one hundred miles off course, a fact I found hard to accept considering all the latest navigation equipment they had on board.

As it turned out, I didn't have to do anything about the compensation. The next day a large force of NVA moved east down the road towards Khe Sanh with tanks. 'Elephant' outpost was wiped out and the villages destroyed. I heard later that most of the male villagers were pressed into forced labor crews to maintain roads.

History revealed the NVA movement towards Khe Sanh was a feint, intended to keep General Westmoreland convinced the big Tet offensive was going to be concentrated there. In that respect, it worked. For the little, peaceful, civilization wiped out in the process, it was a disaster.

Another incident involved a pair of F-4s. It wasn't strictly a short round but it did cost us one F-4 that 'shot itself down.' I was airborne, supporting a First Division (ARVN) sweep near the 'Street Without Joy' area, about three or four miles southeast of Luong Mai, a recently abandoned RF outpost.

One of the elements ran into some strong VC resistance and had been pinned down. They wanted air. The only support available right then were a pair of F-4s with bombs and 20mm guns. They were overhead in minutes. The target area was small and the bombs would have to be right on target to do any good; not a strong possibility with F-4s. My plan was to get the bombs off both of them first then hose the area with 20mm. The rounds are explosive and very effective on lightly dug-in troops.

I put 'lead' in first. He was an old pro and did very well but his bombs were not close enough to do much damage. I asked him to hold high while I put 'two' on the target. 'Two' had problems; a hard time seeing me and my smoke to start with. He was poorly oriented and obviously rattled. It was an easy target – no anti-aircraft guns and only small arms fire. Weather was clear and twenty miles visibility. The ground was flat.

The people on the ground were clamoring for air support. I was trying. 'Lead' broke in to let me know it was 'Two's' first mission so I explained things again very carefully. The heading for the bomb drop was very important since there were several friendly combat elements in the area and I didn't want the fighters going over them on the target approach or departure. Also, exact target position was very important since the pinned down friendlies were only two hundred meters from the enemy.

Finally, I thought he had all the numbers right and the target in sight so I cleared him to start his first pass. To my amazement, he flew right past the right roll-in point, circled the target until he was ninety degrees from the desired approach heading, then rolled in at a very low angle. I told him not to drop, to go around and try again on the correct heading.

He pulled up and made a large circle while I marked the target again with another smoke rocket, then I waited until he was in about the right position and told him to "roll in NOW."

As far out as he was, I thought he'd stay high then dive, but he started down at a very low angle again, about fifteen degrees. He was lined up well, the marking smoke was still over the target so I let him come. At that low angle, the possibility of good bombs was insignificant but, long or short, they wouldn't hurt any friendlies so I cleared him to drop.

I thought he'd release about the time he came by me but I was wrong. He kept going lower and lower. About the time I realized he was too low, he dropped. The bombs had instant fuses; shrapnel tore into the plane. He managed to pull up but his F-4 was losing parts and definitely in bad shape. I yelled for him to eject but it was probably very apparent to the pilot and radar man that they needed a new airplane. Two chutes blossomed at about three hundred feet and they were down in a rice paddy within seconds.

Now we had two problems: the pinned-down ARVN troops and rescuing the crew. Luck was with me. One of the MACV support Huey pilots who just happened to be making a run from Quang Tri to Hue was tuned in on the Division frequency when I started looking for a helicopter. He knew where the abandoned outpost was and headed for it. I circled over the crew until he had me in sight. Less than ten minutes after ejection, they were in a helicopter and headed for home.

The ground troops solved their problem themselves, with mortars and artillery. It was not one of the Air Force's better displays of close air support.

I saw that F-4 tail sticking out of the rice paddy many times after that day. It was an expensive monument. The fighter squadron commander thought it was my fault for continuing to work 'Two' after it was apparent he was having problems. He said I should have told 'Two' to drop his bombs out in the gulf and go home – the wisdom of hindsight. I wondered who had cleared the pilot as 'combat ready.'

Chapter 7

TET

Thanksgiving, Christmas and New Year's Day in Hue had been treated like all the other days, except for changes in the mess hall menu. There was talk of a 'truce' over Christmas but we flew our missions just like any other day. When Tet approached, there was more talk of a truce but most of us weren't sure about the idea of letting down our guard. The possibility of a little vacation from war, even a few moments where we could relax, was appealing. Trusting your enemy, however, would have to be a little stupid. Yet, both sides were Vietnamese and both celebrated Tet, so maybe, just possibly, the truce could be valid. I didn't know who, if anyone, negotiated those truce periods. Most likely they were unilateral declarations, hoping the other side would believe them. Nothing in previous history or current intelligence guaranteed a peaceful Tet but the ARVN planned to reduce its readiness over the holiday.

Pre-Tet parties were hum-dingers. I attended two of them. Gen. Truong was the host for one. A traditional Vietnamese orchestra, dressed in red and gold robes, stood outside the French villa-styled building on the Perfume River bank, sending its music in through open windows. Most of the players were elderly, sixty or seventy years old. Some had long thin beards, down to their waists. Perhaps they had played for the emperor too.

A VNAF detachment that supported the First ARVN Division invited all the Air Force FACs to their party. We chipped in to help with expenses. Part of the ritual was killing a cow and slicing it into bacon-thin strips. Several fifty-five gallon drums had been split in two lengthwise. Half of one was filled with a coal black, viscous mixture of spices and liquids that seemed to produce its own heat. Other half-drums held charcoal fires covered by coarse screen grills.

The idea was to pick up a meat strip with a little bamboo spear, drag it through the black goop until the desired degree of flavor was acquired, then drop it on the grill. When it was done, a highly subjective decision, you ate it. Defense for the roaring fire the food created in your stomach consisted of drinking a lot of whatever was at hand. Late in the evening I went back to the barbecue area for one more piece of 'black death' only to find out there wasn't any meat left. A few brave (spelled fool-hardy) souls were running their hands through the sauce, trying to find meat strips that had come off the bamboo spears while being marinated. I'd had a few drinks but I wasn't that drunk.

Next morning, one of the FACs showed me a right forearm missing most of its hair. And to think we were putting that stuff in our stomachs! I still don't think we ate the whole cow. As always in Vietnam, some skimming had been done.

At midnight on Tet eve, it sounded like almost every gun in Vietnam was emptied into the sky. Machine guns, tracers, flares, everything that could make noise or light was fired. In China, they used firecrackers to chase away the devils. That night in Vietnam, they were shot down.

Millions of dollars went up into the sky and close to every penny probably came from the good old U.S. taxpayer. Little did I realize how much noisier it would get about twenty-four hours later.

After some difficulty getting an airplane (maintenance problems), I took off for my usual flight out to A Shau valley next morning, the first day of the Tet holidays. Weather was a low overcast sky with haze. It didn't look too good but you never know unless you try so I headed for a low place in the first ridge to see if it would be possible to squeeze through without giving anyone an easy shot.

One part of reconnaissance is to look for anything different, any changes in appearance. During my nine months in country, I'd never seen a soul on the network of old trails that spread out across the gently sloping land from the west corner of Hue towards the first ridge and into the jungle. I thought they were made by Montagnards who had lived out there. As months went by without the trails being used, grass grew over them.

I didn't see any people on the trails that morning but the grass was gone. The trails were light tan and wide; every trace of green was gone. That meant a lot of people had walked over those trails during the night!

I continued towards the ridge but it didn't take long to see that there was no way to get out to A Shau that morning.

Besides, the trails were much more interesting. I turned around and went back to the west corner of Hue.

If so many people had gone over those trails, where were they now? The land between Hue and the ridge was covered with high grass and low bushes, very few trees. I looked around the buildings and went back and forth over the area. Nothing.

I landed and drove over to Division Headquarters. No ARVN personnel were around except a duty officer who spoke no English and a few clerks. Col. Adams (Col. Keeler's replacement) was there but he didn't seem particularly interested in what I had seen. I filed an intelligence report through Air Force channels and headed back to the compound. Most of the army advisors were taking it easy since their ARVN counterparts weren't working.

I wanted the ARVN alerted but no one with authority could be reached. In the late afternoon I took off again to see if anything was happening out there. It was very hazy. Visibility was down to about one mile and the ceiling about five hundred feet – too low for me. I parked the plane and headed for the mess hall.

No rock combo, no hi-fi system, no horn, nothing in our day-to-day world makes as much noise as rocket, mortar or artillery shells exploding near you. I like hi-fi systems and had built one huge enclosure containing sixteen large co-axial speakers. It was in the basement at home waiting for my return. The thing took more power to make it work well than my amplifier had at the time but maybe, if I had a good recording of an attack and could afford a new amplifier, I might be able to let others experience the noise but not the danger (except for ear drums).

I had bought a little Japanese recorder with an auxiliary battery power supply. Almost every night before going to bed, I put on a long-playing tape and set it up to record by just flipping one switch. Unfortunately, I'd either forgotten to put the tape on or start the recorder during previous attacks on the compound. That night I remembered to set it up.

The NVA gunners were good. The first rocket, a 122 millimeter, landed on the roof of the province chief's command post. My room was on the second floor, right across a narrow street from the command post so the blast was big enough to tell me it was going to be an extra special night.

One of my authorized pieces of equipment was a USAF jeep loaded with radios to use when I accompanied the Division on ground operations. My duty position during attacks on the compound was in the command post (CP) with my jeep close by to request or direct air support such as flare ships and spookys.

As soon as the echoes of the first rocket died down I started to get dressed and head for the CP. A rocket hit in the barbed wire along our side of the street between compounds. Luckily, the door jamb was lined up between the rocket and me. Shrapnel and pieces of barbed wire peppered the walls and woodwork on both sides but only a few objects hit me on my chest, arms and hands, probably glass from the windows. I was only aware of one cut on my left hand for some time.

Several vehicles parked along the fence caught fire so I had plenty of light to turn on the recorder, put a dressing on my hand and find a flight suit. I grabbed my roommate's M-16 (he was in Australia on R & R and mine had been destroyed at Khe Sanh) and headed for the command post. Not knowing if, when or where the next rocket would hit, the trip was in the Russian roulette category.

I'd been in the command post only a few minutes when someone with a bloody face came in and yelled that the troops in the VIP house were in a bad way and needed help. I ran over.

One B-40 round had hit a through-the-wall air conditioner and blew parts all over the room. Several men were wounded. Another B-40 had hit the guard tower by the corner of the house and one man was critically wounded. It appeared the attackers were going to try penetrating the compound at that corner. Col. Keeler was right.

It was pitch black out there – thick clouds and fog. Reinforcements arrived in bunches. We were pumping so much lead down that street I couldn't see how anyone out there could live. Somehow we had to keep their heads down while the wounded guard was extracted from the tower. About that time, someone asked for flares. I headed for my radio jeep.

No way. The jeep was parked by the fence, not far from the burning vehicles. It would be suicide to go out there, well-lighted by the fire. Besides, it had flat tires and other visible damage. Back in the command post, I was wondering what to do when a phone rang. Much to my surprise, the NVA had not cut the lines. I called the Direct Air Support Center in Da Nang and explained that we needed a flare ship right away. The person who answered was polite but didn't believe me when I described the conditions in Hue. All I could get was a promise to try to send a flare ship. It didn't come. Dawn finally did.

The NVA couldn't have picked better weather for their Tet attack at Hue. Except for a few short breaks some afternoons, the first four days were solid low overcast with haze or fog; no possibility for Spooky's mini-guns. We did get excellent support with flare ships after the first night.

Things calmed down later in the morning so I went up to my room to check the tape recorder. It had run the whole reel through so I flipped it over and started a series of tapes describing the first few days in the battle for Hue.

(At this point I suggest the reader play a copy of the tape or read Appendix A which is a transcript of the tapes. [see page 162])

I didn't feel particularly useful in the compound after three or four days. Our Marines had arrived and were gradually, at a terrible cost in lives and wounds, re-taking city territory south of the Perfume River. A landing zone (LZ) had been cleared in a small park between the province chief's compound and the south bank of the Perfume. Things weren't going too well on the other side of the river so I decided to go over to Division Headquarters and see if the Air Force could help Gen. Truong and his troops. The Army set up a slick (Huey without door gunners) to carry me over and said it would hit the LZ in a few minutes.

I stuffed a few essentials (toilet paper and C-rations) in a kit bag, handed my tapes to a FAC and asked him to put them in the mail when he got to Da Nang, then headed for the LZ. Someone had blown a hole in the Province Chief's compound wall opposite our gate so people could get to the LZ without going out on the street.

Chapter 8

TET, THE OTHER SIDE OF TOWN

The first thing I noticed when walking out of the province chief's compound gate towards the LZ was that no one was standing up. Except for some wounded on stretchers and body bags, everyone was in fox-holes or behind something solid. A sergeant that appeared to be in charge of the LZ waved me towards a fox-hole.

Fighting was intense directly across the river in downtown Hue. I couldn't see any troops but artillery was shelling buildings along the canal which heads northeast from the Perfume River through the business district.

Rounds were zipping into the park where I was as well as across the river and I decided this was what they called a hot LZ. A badly wounded Marine was lying on a stretcher just a few feet from me. He was motionless except for his eyes. They were moving quite a lot, as though he was trying to orient himself. I felt very sorry for him, bad wounds, lying out there on the open ground when I'm snug in a fox-hole. I tried to think of something to say that would cheer him up besides, "How's it going, Buddy?" It was obvious things weren't going very well.

His eyes stopped moving. I waited. They didn't move. I waited. A medic was crouched down over another wounded Marine. I waved and pointed to the guy next to me and indicated he might be dead. The medic came over, in a crouch, check for vital signs, pulled a piece of cloth over the Marine's head and left.

I sat in the fox-hole and took in the scene. Well, I thought, his troubles are over but who's going to cry for him at home? Who's going to get the bad news: mother, father, brothers, sisters, wife, children, friends? I became a little bitter as I looked at the violently torn flesh on the stretcher. Would the United States or his family be any better off for his sacrifice over here on the other side of the world? Not likely, I thought.

A motion in the background brought my attention back to the immediate situation. It was the LZ sergeant waving from his position behind some felled palm tree trunks. Explosions across the river died down for a few seconds and he yelled that my bird would be in shortly. I knew that the Huey would attract all sorts of fire (mortars, rockets, bullets, etc.) so minimum ground time was essential. It was obvious the pilot knew it was hot too. He came in low and fast over the compound behind me and was in final descent in seconds.

I was out of the fox-hole and running before he touched and belly-flopped into the back end just as his runners hit the ground. It was an instant up and away. He was accelerating so rapidly it was hard to roll over and sit up. I grabbed a strap on the back of the cabin and pulled myself up so I could see where we were going. Shit! We were staying low and headed directly towards the canal, where firing and shelling was the heaviest.

Helicopters are noisy, especially Hueys with all doors open and rapidly accelerating to top speed. Both pilots were wearing helmets. There was no one else in back and not enough time to move forward and get their attention. I yelled "Go left! Go left!" at the top of my lungs. I could feel pain in my throat but I could hardly hear myself. No chance he could hear me. It was obvious; I was simply going for a short ride with no influence on the route so I turned towards the open door and became a spectator.

It was wild. He stayed very low while crossing the Perfume. As we pulled up over the bridge at the mouth of the canal, I saw soldiers in doorways and on rooftops pointing their guns at us but we were so low and going so fast I didn't feel like a sitting duck. Aiming and firing my M-16 was impossible so there wasn't anything constructive to do. I could have waved but that probably wouldn't have meant too much to them.

The helicopter had an intermittent vibration as if someone was hitting the bottom with a sledge hammer – thump, thump. I leaned out and looked around. The runners were hitting the trees. Wow! That's flying! Doing a hundred and twenty knots with your runners in the trees takes skill, guts and a cool head.

He turned a little to the left where the canal turned right and a few seconds later we were over the First Division compound. When we landed I ran around to the front of the Huey and gave the pilot a salute, with feeling.

He took off immediately for another destination. No words had passed between us. I looked at the trip as an adventure; he probably looked at it as an errand. People can get used to anything. I hope he survived.

The first thing I did was go upstairs at Division headquarters and say hello to S/Sgt. Pursey, one of my radio operators. I had a communications center there for relaying air strike requests from FACs and other information to and from the Direct Air Support Center (DASC) and squadron headquarters, using both radios and telephones. The center was manned twenty-four hours a day. Sgt. Pursey happened to be the operator on duty at the start of the attack so he had been stuck there four days. I wondered what he'd been eating, for one thing.

Except for a scraggly beard, he was in fine shape, existing on a mixture of Vietnamese army issue rice sweetened with odds and ends of C-rations. The rice ration was a neat set-up; a resealable plastic bag with dry, cooked rice inside. All you did was pour boiling water inside, reseal the bag for a few minutes and, presto, you had a meal of sorts. Open a can of C-rations and drop it in the bag too and you had something like 'chicken breast on rice pilaf', with a little imagination.

Sanitary conditions in the ARVN compound were terrible. There was no running water but the troops had continued to use the flush toilets. When the commodes had filled up, they used the floor around them and then the hallway in front of the toilets. Flies were thick and I thought about what they had been walking on before they landed on me. It was a disease exchange area, not a place of convenience.

I held my bowel movements for two days, suggesting to several ARVN officers that the place needed cleaning. Nothing happened. Gen. Truong had plenty of problems much greater than mine but the time of 'critical mass' was approaching. I was not going to drop my pants and poop on the parade ground. There were three U.S. Army advisors in the compound. I asked them where they were 'going' and the answers were that they weren't. Finally, I mentioned the problem to Gen. Truong and a miracle happened – the place was cleaned up in a few hours and a barrel of water from the moat moved in for flushing by bucket. Relief at last! A lot of other things happened during those days in the ARVN compound but physical discomfort is the first thing that comes to mind. Pain makes a deep impression.

The situation in and around the Citadel wasn't good. Gen. Truong had put his best troops to work clearing the area but progress was very slow. The NVA had dug in, digging trenches and converting buildings into strong defensive positions. The top of the Palace and outer walls had been fortified with a network of trenches and bunkers. Artillery type support was available to the NVA in the form of 122mm rockets, mortars and B-40s. Continued bad weather made close air support impossible. The presence of friendly civilians throughout the area complicated matters as well. Progress was measured in inches and lives.

Days were long, nights were longer. ARVN troops, with good reason, had a reputation for changing sides when things got tight. I wasn't at all certain that they would remain loyal.

Most of them were outside the compound wall. If the NVA opened the gate some night and said, "Surprise, you're mine", there was little the three advisors and I could do about it. Being captured or killed did not appeal to me.

Several months back, a young army lieutenant told me about his experience with Vietnamese military personnel. He was the U.S. advisor for an RF manned outpost guarding Highway One and a small village about twenty miles south of Hue. One night, the outpost was attacked using the typical mortar then ground assault pattern. As soon as the shelling stopped, he started out to check troop positions. To his amazement, the front gate was wide open and he was alone. In a matter of minutes, he saw VC running into the compound. It was time to hide, but where? He ran into a shed where his jeep and supply trailer were parked. Voices and footsteps were approaching. He draped himself over the tire on his trailer, the side closest to the wall, and squeezed between the tire and the fender. Fortunately, he had a small body.

Seconds later the VC were in the shed. They were calling for him by name, in English. They used phrases like "Lt. Sullivan, where are you?" and "Come out, Lt. Sullivan." One climbed into the empty trailer and bounced it up and down while calling his name. Fender braces were stabbing his back but he didn't complain out loud.

No one came around to his side of the trailer and after a while, they left. Most of the troops wandered back in the next morning and work went on – 'guarding' the area.

I felt things could be the same there. Mortars and rockets were hitting in the compound day and night, there were many casualties and support just wasn't coming like we felt it should. Sometimes at night it became very quiet and I wondered if we were alone. Somehow the General and his staff held things together.

The low point in my personal morale came one night when we were alerted by radio that a formation of North Vietnamese aircraft were headed south towards the DMZ. The anticipated target was Hue. It was the first time I felt a sincere desire to be someplace else. They didn't arrive. My morale recovered.

I was pleased to hear that our Marines made it to House Eight on Tuesday, the sixth, and returned all the airmen to the MACV compound. After a few days, Division troops had made good progress southeast towards the downtown area but only a few short blocks to the west. It was an area of small to medium size residences, the airport and elementary schools. Enemy troops were dug in on the Citadel walls, plus many positions in buildings made with heavy brick and concrete walls – excellent shelters from small arms fire.

Defensive troops can pick their spots, get ideal fields of fire. Advancing troops must move between sheltered positions and have few opportunities to set up good fields of fire. Movement and firing from inadequate positions involves more risks, more casualties. It was murder out there.

Up to that point, rules of engagement had prevented the Air Force from providing any significant support in the Hue battle. No ordnance could be dropped in the city, suburbs or tomb areas unless Gen. Truong specifically requested it.

By Wednesday, February 7, Gen. Truong was looking for any help available. Weather was still bad so typical close air support missions were impossible. I suggested 'sky spots' and carefully explained what we could do for him.

Sky spots were bomb drops from fighters flying level at high altitude. Release point was determined by 'bomb scoring' computer/ radar installations that were worked in reverse. During SAC training missions in the states, bomb drops were simulated using a radio tone to indicate drop time. A radar scoring site near the designated target would take the various factors (aircraft altitude, speed, direction, etc.) into consideration and calculate where a bomb would have hit. They were precise and reliable systems.

Several installations had been moved to South Vietnam and set up to work backwards. Target coordinates and desired heading to the release point were established in advance. The site would direct the fighter pilot by radio while watching his actions on radar then telling him when to drop. The controllers' directions to the pilot (details left out) would sound something like this:

"I have your aircraft positively identified; turn right 210 degrees; your course to release point will be 245 degrees; you are coming up on course; turn right to 245 degrees; you are drifting off course to left; turn right to 248 degrees; you are back on course; turn left to 246 degrees; holding course nicely; release point in ten seconds; five, four, three, two, one, drop." The pilot usually released all bombs at once and headed for home.

I didn't know what the real accuracy was on sky spots. I usually predicted that they would hit within a one hundred by two hundred meter box centered on the target and aligned with the approach heading. So far I hadn't seen a wild sky spot bomb and the average accuracy on those I had given BDAs was close to my predictions. I gave Gen. Truong those figures.

He and his staff talked it over. I knew what they were concerned about: civilians, the palace, NVA positions, intelligence reports, perhaps even where their own families were. Finally they took my map of the Hue area and put four 'X's' on it, along the inside of the southwest wall. That's where they wanted the first bombs. I worked out a drop course where long or short bombs would be least likely to land on friendlies and explained it to them. The general nodded his head; go.

Sgt. Pursey and I both encoded the coordinates and cross-checked our results before transmitting the request. Someone in the DASC checked the coordinates and found they were within the city. About a half-hour later Sgt. Pursey received a message: "Sky spots would not be approved unless strike request forms were signed by Gen. Truong." My God! Here we were at war, a bad situation and they are thinking SYA, all the way. I called Col. Baker and protested. "Isn't my name on the request good enough?" The answer was no. It had to be Gen. Truong's.

I handed the strike request form to Gen. Truong with an apology. He was a good man; he understood and signed the meaningless form without hesitation.

About 10:00 P.M. I got the word – all four strikes were approved and they would be put in starting about 2:00 A.M. All the aircraft would be carrying seven hundred, fifty pound bombs with delayed fuses, as requested. They make big holes and throw trash a long way. Just what we needed for fortified positions.

This was going to be interesting. I'd never been this close (on the ground) to a bomb drop before. The time I got caught in a B-52 strike was different; while I was close, it was daylight, I was in the air and not expecting anything. This time maybe I could hear the bombs coming and feel what it was like to be a near miss. Also, I was concerned about accuracy so I plotted the azimuth from the south balcony of the command post to the first target. If the first strike was off too much, I'd call a halt.

Sgt. Pursey and I killed time until about 1:45, then he set up his UHF radio to the sky spot channel. Our radio room was on the north side of the building but a cross corridor was close so we could get to the south side in seconds. The first flight contacted sky spot on time and work began. The planes were high; I think it was eighteen thousand feet. We'd have plenty of time to get in position to observe the impact point. As usual, the night was pitch black, with a low overcast sky, no stars, no moon, no lights of any kind. I wouldn't be able to see a compass or any buildings but I knew the approximate angle from the balcony railing and that would have to be good enough.

The first 'drop' command came within seconds of 2:00 A.M. We rushed through the corridor to the south side and waited, staring into total blackness.

First I heard a faint rushing sound, like a lady in a silk dress moving behind you. I wasn't sure at first but the sound increased rapidly and then there was no doubt – it was them! Before I expected it, there was a big white noiseless flash right where I was looking while the rushing sound continued to increase; then the shock wave hit us – bal-l-l-l-l-a-m-m-m-m-m! The violence was tremendous. How could anyone survive in that area?

Gen. Truong and his staff liked the sky spots; they were on target or close enough to do a lot of damage. I'm sure it made the enemy troops in fortified positions pucker up a little.

There were a lot of intelligence reports coming in via civilians and agents regarding locations of VC/NVA troops, fortifications and supply points in and around the city. The best targets were saved for sky spots. Starting on February 7, I set up an average of three or four strikes a night for a week.

Any doubt about the effectiveness of intelligence-targeted sky spot bombs in this battle was erased early Thursday morning, the eighth, when a reported ammo dump went up in a spectacular secondary explosion. The strike was in an area called Hau Thon, on the west edge of town.

Late in the evening of the ninth, we received a report of a large concentration of enemy troops resting inside the wall, near the Cua An Hoa gate, just one thousand meters from us. Gen. Truong wanted us to hit them hard. I had several sky spot flights already set up with 750 pound bombs that would be launching soon. The best possibility was to divert one of them to the new target. The only problem was the fuses: all were equipped with time delay – good for fortified positions but not so good for troops on the surface.

Through an encrypted message exchange, we convinced the DASC that a new hot target required instant fuses and we'd take a delay to get them. Somewhere armament men were called out in the wee hours to replace the fuses and a couple of fighter jockeys had to sit around a dull ready-room waiting for the job to be done. I hoped they weren't too unhappy, but war is hell.

The planes didn't get there until about five o'clock in the morning but that was okay. It was still pitch black and I doubted if there had been any significant troop movements. Sgt. Pursey and I did our routine: listen for the drop command then head for the balcony. This drop was by far the closest to our position and the instant fuses should make a difference in what we'd see and hear.

I didn't realize how much difference there would be. We could hear them coming much better, the flashes were brilliant. It looked like everything between us and the explosions were X-rayed. The shock waves blew us back from the railing. Concussion broke a few window panes behind us. Wow!

After the echoes died away, I heard activity in the room behind us. Soon I was surrounded by several upset U.S. Army advisors who had been sleeping there. They had all sorts of questions about what was going on. I told them we had a hot target over by the gate. Then they got mad at me for not waking them up, gently, before the strike. I thought it was rather funny but nothing they said tended to support my conclusion.

People were hurting and dying all over the place and I was standing there in the dark trying not to laugh. I couldn't think about them; it would drive me nuts.

As soon as that area of Hue had been retaken, I took my city map (which I still have) and drove over to several of the strike areas, looked around and took some pictures. None had hit within the Imperial Palace walls and accuracy was well within the one hundred by two hundred meter box I had described.

Later I learned from the ARVN that ten children had been hiding in a school building that was leveled by one of my skyspots. I was told the strikes did shake up the NVA forces in some areas and made those positions easier to retake. Who's to know what's right? I could have rationalized and debated those decisions forever. No conclusions are valid in anything but the environment at that time – is it them or us, him or me? The only thing I'm sure about now is that the whole war, or at least our participation, was regrettable.

Some direct quotes from my letters to Janice, written while I was at Division, might prove more interesting than recounting the events. Fatigue lowered my standards for correspondence and the only paper available was a scratch pad. They took the form of a dairy since I couldn't mail them when written. My account of activities at Division is based on memory and those letters. Janice had filed them away and twenty-two years later, when I needed them, they were available. All quotes are exactly as written:

February 10: "The average temperature since this whole affair started has been 55 degrees at night and 65 as the high each day. With no heat, no windows, the net result is a perpetual chill. Some guys are getting colds but so far, I've stayed healthy. I'm wearing all the clothes I have, including the flight jacket you sent. It's not stylish and not clean but reasonably warm.

"Of the fifteen Air Force people here at the start, five have been wounded (including me). Airman Rose got shot in the foot yesterday. (I found out later he'd shot himself to qualify for a medivac.) Slowly but steadily, I'm getting them out to Da Nang. There are only a few left and we probably won't go lower until the mess at the airport can be cleaned up and equipment salvaged."

February 11: "Another day – the weather is the best for ten days – eleven hundred foot overcast. My O-2s are flying over the city but nobody else. I get mad when – well, hell, it is still pretty hot around here and I guess the Army and Marines would rather not . . .

"The thing is I've had Army pilots refer to my FACs as fair weather fliers, yet who's missing when it's hot and the weather's not?

"Whoops! Things had been dull around for the past three days, then all of a sudden, we just got about ten 82mm mortar rounds. Now the 'experts' say they were rockets, one major says they were artillery – who knows? They were loud. One truck is burning. I haven't heard of any wounded. This building has a heavy concrete roof and as long as you are inside, it's no sweat.

"Well, I got tired of all the guessing so, taking Sgt. Pursey with me, we went out and dug up a crater. We found a rocket motor – 122mm. I looked up the range, estimated the direction from the crater angle and sent a FAC out to look. One site has been located and, well, we'll do *something*. Total damage was one truck destroyed and one wounded – not much results for all the efforts."

February 12: "Once again the Marines have landed – only five tanks but two companies of troops are coming today (I hope) and *then* maybe things will get moving. It appears that 'Charlie' has pretty much left the area, leaving only a few to slow recovery. They are in well-fortified areas and will take a lot of rooting out.

"Last night I gave my estimate of several situations to one of the G-3 (operations) officers. He told someone else and, well, it grew until we had what was a battle conference including the Deputy Commander. As has happened before, they had become immersed in concern only for the immediate situation in Hue and I went over the other enemy movements we had reported in the week prior to the attack. I was surprised how well they listened and bought my recommendations. I'm sure Gen. Truong will get briefed today. I wouldn't be surprised if our discussion would materially change their tactics. Basically, I said that regardless of the military outcome of this battle, the VC had achieved a political victory. That it was important to reduce fighting in the populated areas; that they should pick a position in the interior that was of strategic value to the VC and occupy it. This would draw the main forces from the flat-lands. If they picked

Ta Bat, they could stop supply traffic into and through A Shau Valley as well as tie up troops; that they must attack and force the enemy to follow his movements; disorganize the attack plans of the VC; that *they would lose* the two northern-most provinces if they remain on the defensive; that they can *never* win if they remain in fortified positions on the defensive.

"I went over these points in detail several times as more became interested and I predict they will follow my recommendations. They were surprised how much I knew about their provinces but I reminded them that I had been in the air between five and six hundred hours." (ARVN and U.S. forces re-entered A Shau Valley during May, 1968, near Ta Bat.)

"The fighting by the ARVNs has just about stopped. They have loose control over about half of the area inside and *none* of the area outside. Artillery, mortar and bombs are our only activity (much of that) and rockets and mortars the only enemy activity. I've been saying there are less than two hundred VC left in the walled city area. But no one will move to find out how many remain.

"We hear that some stores are open down town and people are moving around fairly freely. If so, and the ARVN stay holed up for days, then they will lose all respect of the civilians.

"In summary – situation not good; not dangerous but not good.

"Just got a radio call telling me to be at a meeting at Da Nang tomorrow – after recovering my composure I advised Da Nang that I would be more than glad to attend if they could arrange transportation.

"Despite daily phone calls, they just aren't aware of the situation here.

"It's amazing what you can get used to – I use my flak jacket for a pillow; I can wash and shave in one helmet of water; the mirror on a jeep is just fine to shave by; when you are tired, that canvas cot with no mattress looks as good as a Simmons Beauty-Rest; cooking rice over a candle and mixing it up with C-rations makes a delicious meal; you can go for days without changing sox or even taking your shoes off; mortar shells dropping into your compound are considered a minor irritant; cigarette tobacco works pretty good in a pipe; toilet paper is the *most* important thing; physical possessions aren't nearly as important as security; etc.

"Anyway, it's a different sort of life than I've been used to but it is relatively easy to adapt.

"Still have the stitches in my hand. Got to get to a doctor and see when they should come out."

February 14: "Better weather today. Got about twelve airstrikes in. VNAF, Marine and Air Force combined. Coordinating the activities of ARVN, Vietnamese marines and USMC and their air requirements really kept me busy – crises by the dozen." (End letter quotes.)

Things improved a lot more rapidly on the south side of the Perfume, thanks to our Marines. The Thua Thien FACs had gone back to Da Nang and were flying missions out of there. The Quang Tri FACs had survived quite well and were back flying missions out of their gravel air strip. I was the only one still on the ground.

Maj. Goss, one of my province ALOs, was sent up to replace me on the fifteenth of February. He had a message. I was to see my boss in Da Nang as soon as possible. Late that afternoon I bummed a helicopter ride back to the compound. It was still exciting but not as wild as the ride over.

My roommate had been in Australia on R and R when the NVA hit Hue. He didn't get back until after I'd moved to the First Division headquarters. When I came back for a clean-up before answering my summons to Da Nang, he was not at all pleasant. I found out why.

The two rooms we shared had ceiling fans – big heavy cast iron things with wooden blades. They hung from sturdy hooks in the ceiling. Sometime during the first few days, concussion from a tank gun or some other big explosion shook the building so bad the fan in the bedroom jumped off the hook. It shattered when it hit the concrete floor. I threw out the pieces and cleaned up both rooms. Plaster, glass, screen, barbed wire, shrapnel and plaster chips had really made a big mess. Sometime after I left and before he returned, the other fan was blown off its hook.

I had finished assembling a giant plastic model of the Saturn moon rocket system the night before the Tet attack. It was sitting in the middle of our coffee table, directly under the fan. When the fan came down, plastic pieces and fan parts flew all over the room. He thought I'd left the big mess for him to clean up.

Next morning, after a two-quart bath and a haircut, after making a tape for my wife, I started looking for transportation to Da Nang.

By some mysterious means, a helicopter appeared just to get me down there. I thought, "I must have really screwed up if they want me there this bad." I was used to hitching rides or flying myself down.

My boss, Col. Black, was standing there waiting when the helicopter flared for landing. Something didn't check out – I expected him to be scowling but he was smiling – hardly a prelude to a chewing. The first thing he said was, "You shaved!" Twenty-four hours later I was in Hong Kong. The good Colonel had set me up for a little R and R. Nice guy. I like bosses who do things like that. It is called consideration.

I had read about people having problems adjusting from primary survival objectives in Vietnam to a secure environment in the States within a matter of hours. It was good to be in a more peaceful part of the world and worry about little things like, "Shall I have steak or chops?" In Hong Kong my only problem was loud, unexpected noises. I tended to duck first, then look.

While in Hong Kong, I bought a car. The U.S. Navy had a big exchange there and, among other things, you could order cars for delivery most anywhere at wholesale prices. I picked out a Plymouth and set the delivery date in Kansas City for a week after my tour of duty was over. The company handling the transaction was from West Germany. After I got home and picked up the car, I headed for the county courthouse in Papillion, Nebraska to get the car titled and licensed. I handed the clerk a handful of papers. She shuffled through them, frowned, went through them again, then came back to the window wanting a little explanation. "Where did you buy the car?" "Hong Kong." "Where were you stationed?" "Vietnam." "Who did you buy it from?" "International Autoworks, West Germany." "Where did you take possession?" "Kansas City." "Where do you live?" "Bellevue." Eventually, I got the title.

After five days in Hong Kong, it was back to war. By then Hue proper was secure, the railroad bridge made usable by bulldozing a ramp down to the end dropped by NVA sappers and many shops back in business. Fire-fights still occurred in the outskirts as clearing forces ran into pockets of resistance.

Every airplane on the field had been destroyed by satchel charges except for one O-1. It stood there in the middle of all that wreckage with only a bent rudder and a few shrapnel and bullet holes. I thought it had been booby-trapped but a careful inspection didn't reveal any bomb. Mechanics took the wings off in preparation for airlifting it by helicopter back to Da Nang. Next morning the wings were gone; someone had stolen them, probably for materials with which to fashion some sort of waterproof roof. People were desperate for anything to provide some shelter from wind and rain. We didn't look for them very hard.

Atrocities much worse than a dirty room started being uncovered. Our mama-san (maid) was an older woman who spoke excellent French. A few of the Vietnamese people who had been working in the compound began to return. They had long faces. I asked one I knew if she had seen our mama-san. She shook her head and said, "She no come back." I checked further and found one of the workers had seen her, hands tied behind her back, in a group being marched by VC towards the east side of the city, where some of the mass burial sites had been found. It was likely that she had been killed; a fifty-year old woman guilty of working for Americans. I was told by a Vietnamese officer that about three thousand bodies were located in mass graves. It appeared that many had been buried alive.

Three German doctors, two men and one woman, lived in the University district of Hue and taught in the medical school. They were volunteers, helping the Vietnamese people. We welcomed their occasional visits to the MACV compound. They considered American beer superior to Vietnamese and we were happy to provide it. We were concerned about their fate during the first attack. The Marines found them, hands tied behind their backs, bullet holes through their heads. What a waste! What political system, political philosophy could rationalize killing people in their category? In the long run, no social system could succeed that is so stupid. There is no suitable substitute for thinking.

I noticed the door frame on the room next to mine had some damage. One of the Army majors who lived in that room told me what happened. He was talking with another guy while a pitch battle was going on across the Perfume, sitting on his bed, leaning back against the inside wall. Suddenly there was a violent 'whap' and the room filled with splinters. A second later, before he could react, an object dropped on the bed beside him. He felt the thump and looked down. An image hit the retina of his eyes. It was transmitted to his brain via small changes in ion balances within the short optic nerves. The brain went to work sorting out and processing the information in a marvelous series/parallel network of neurons and synapses, built for speed.

Several questions had to be decided, based on the image received: A: What had landed beside this huge mass of living cells arranged in symbiotic relationships, commonly referred to as a human body? Answer: A smoking hot anti-tank round.

B: Was it dangerous to the health of the group? Answer: Yes.

C: What was the best course of action to preserve health?

Answer: Place feet on floor somewhere near the center of gravity of the cell group and thrust upwards, then continue to accelerate the mass through reciprocating motions of the lower extremities until it was out of the beat-up door and some distance away from the object observed.

That's what he did, probably taking only a few seconds. However, he said it seemed like an eternity between the 'plop' and turning the corner around the door. Everything was in slow motion.

That's war: hours and hours of sheer boredom punctuated by moments of stark terror.

The round didn't explode, probably because deceleration through the wood and plaster door frame wasn't great enough to trip the fuse. It hit the inside wall sideways, not in the right direction to trip the fuse, then landed on a soft bed. Luck.

Lt. Koung (VNAF) was in charge of the airfield inside the Citadel. He was a hard working, pleasant person with a pretty wife and three young children. The field must have been high on the Tet attack hit-list because NVA troops were in the area just about as soon as things got started. People in the little two-room operations shed scattered. One told me Lt. Koung grabbed a case of hand grenades and headed for a fox-hole near the south end of the runway. His body was found there. I hope he took a lot of NVA with him. His family just disappeared.

A satchel charge placed in our refueling system had failed to go off and, by some minor miracle, the fuel bladder, nested in a low trench, hadn't been holed so all we needed was airplanes and rockets to get operational.

My poor radio jeep had been pushed into a corner of the compound, awaiting disposal. It was nothing more than a pile of junk. Shrapnel from one of the first 122mm rockets punctured three tires, one radio and made many holes in the body. A rock shower, fall-out from blowing up a building next to the compound, shredded the top and mashed the hood down on top of the engine. The third or fourth day, a B-40 hit it right at the base of the windshield frame. That powerful, shaped-charge explosion scattered radio parts all over the compound and reduced the back half to torn metal supported by its basic frame.

I walked by one day as it waited for burial, or whatever they did with junk in Vietnam, and felt a pang of sorrow. It had served its nation well in dire times and some recognition seemed appropriate. Maybe hanging a yellow tag on those torn remains would be appropriate. I didn't get around to it. If there is a heaven for all those torn-up jeeps from three wars, I hope it's up there, running around and yakking away, as always.

Tet, like a bad dream, had come and gone. The city was battered and many thousands killed, yet it took only days to become functional again. Shops opened, trade resumed, lights came on, water started running and traffic was moving again. Hue's quick bounce back to vitality was as surprising as the attack.

I liked the way Vietnamese seemed to think. What's done is done. How do we get to where we want to be from where we are? Let's not worry about getting back to where we were. It reminded me of something I learned in missile school: when an ICBM gets pushed off course, say by a high wind during take-off, it doesn't correct back to the initial course. Instead, it calculates a new course directly to the target from where it is. Getting there requires less energy that way.

Chapter 9

FLYING

Mother saved a few of my school drawings from third or fourth grade. Airplanes and boats were in almost every one. From then to now, some sixty years later, nothing has changed; they remain high on my list of interests. Puberty hit me as hard as anyone, mentally undressing every girl and regretting every pimple but never slowing my model airplane building and flying. Times with the opposite sex were important but if one of my models landed in a tree, the girl had to wait.

My first airplane ride was in a Ford Tri-motor. My first night flight was in a giant biplane – a Curtiss Condor. It carried ten or fifteen passengers on a pair of huge wings with two liquid-cooled V-12 engines between them. My sister was a newspaper reporter. She used her status to get me an introduction to the pilot. To my absolute, total and supreme delight, he invited me to sit in the right seat (no co-pilot around) and handed me a flashlight. My duty during the flight was to check the oil pressure on the right engine about every ten minutes. The gauge was on the engine nacelle and positioned so it could be read from the cockpit.

The take-off was awesome. Incredible noise, flames shooting out of red-hot exhaust pipes, streaming well beyond the end of the engine housing. I didn't see how the fabric-covered wings and body could keep from catching on fire but they didn't. I was hooked. Flying was going to be part of my life. Thanks to my father's interest in flying, I got a lot of light-plane rides during my early teens and took my first lesson in an Aeronca C-3 before heading off to college.

Vietnam gave me the opportunity to finish my Air Force career with a burst of flying activity, best of all, in the kind of airplanes I liked and with very little regulation. No flight plans, no paperwork, no formal de-briefings, no supervision. Even with being on the ground for almost a month during the Tet battle, I managed to get over seven hundred hours of flying in O-1s and O-2s plus rides in many other types, including LOCHS (Hughes-produced light observation/combat helicopters), Hueys, C-123s with jet boosters and C-130s.

When I say 'no supervision', I must qualify the statement. No squadron supervisory personnel ever came to Hue or Quang Tri during the year I was there. Other than the customary in-country check-rides when I arrived and a few days of transition training when we received the first O-2s, we were left to ourselves – until a new regime formed at Group Headquarters, down in Can Tho. We heard that flight standardization boards had been set up at Group and Squadron levels. All pilots had to receive standardization check rides every six months.

I couldn't believe it. My God! This was combat; what we had been training for since Korea. Now they had taken pilots off combat duty and made them instructors and we were going to schedule check flights in an all-out combat situation! I objected. Survival and mission effectiveness were the measurements now, not check rides. We were doing very well in both categories, no accidents, no wounded (in the air) or killed and better than ninety percent of all missions completed as scheduled. Nevertheless I lost the argument. One by one, the Quang Tri and Thua Thien FACs dutifully flew down to Da Nang, took their check ride and came back certified for combat, something they'd been doing for months.

Squadron people kept calling me, saying I had to come down and get my check ride too. They knew what I thought about the whole dumb program. It was a dilemma. A square had to be filled, forms completed and mailed to Group Headquarters or they weren't doing a good job in the war. One day the squadron called and said a check pilot was coming up from Da Nang and I was to meet him at the field.

He was a nice guy. We talked. He showed an interest in seeing Hue so we climbed into my jeep and drove around the city for an hour or so. When we returned to the airport, he pulled a form-covered clipboard out of his O-2 and made several marks on it then signed his name. He looked up, smiled and said, "That was a hell of a good check ride. You passed with flying colors." I took a picture to commemorate the very special occasion and he flew back to Da Nang.

The O-1 was a simple airplane. Its honest flight characteristics and my frequent flying pushed me to a state of proficiency where it was like strapping a pair of wings on my back. Handling the plane was almost subconscious; throttle, mixture, flaps, airspeed and controls got to the right positions without check lists. Corrections for cross-winds and turbulence during landings became automatic.

The O-2s, with two engines and some design compromises I didn't like, were a little more of a chore to fly but it was reassuring to have a second fan. Flying a single engine airplane over miles of jungle and mountains without a parachute and nothing but enemy below did involve a degree of faith in mechanical things that strained logical thought at times. Advantages and disadvantages between the O-1s and O-2s were a wash as far as I was concerned. I flew either without regrets.

One of the design decisions in the O-2 I didn't like was the throttle linkage for the rear engine. It consisted of a flexible, push-pull control cable about ten feet long. When everything worked right, there was still a lot of friction and spongy motion in the system. Setting rear engine power involved trial and error.

Early models (we had the first used in Vietnam) had the cable routed too close to an exhaust pipe. On long flights, the heat sometimes baked lubricants in the cable so hard that it would become impossible to open the throttle any farther (a push action) than the setting the pilot had at the time. It wasn't a bad problem because you could usually reduce power for landing by horsing back on the throttle (a pull action). Of course, once you retarded the throttle, you had to fly the rest of the mission with the rear engine idling or shut down and feathered. About the only time it could cause a problem would be during a goofed-up landing.

One night I was flying an O-2 on an airborne alert mission. I flew a route that took me over all the outposts in the province where American advisors were stationed and checked in by radio with each one, just to let them, and the VC, know a FAC was up and available. After that, my flight path was random, towards anything that attracted my interest, such as light flashes (explosions) and tracers.

Every so often, I checked the rear throttle to see if it was getting stiff. It was. I found that thirty seconds of rapid throttle movement between idle and cruise positions would loosen it up again so I set up a schedule. Every fifteen minutes was exercise time for the rear throttle.

I happened to be near the Quang Dien outpost late that night when it was exercise time. A voice came over my FM radio, "Trail 30, this is Blazer Actual, are you having engine problems?" I hadn't thought about what it sounded like outside; one engine running steadily and the other surging rapidly from idle to cruise to idle, etc. My abbreviated explanation didn't seem to satisfy him. I assured him it was no sweat and I'd be up for a while longer. His last message urged me to park the plane and call it a night. I felt he would rather undergo ten mortar attacks than be up there with me. I'd rather have ten flights like that one (no major actions) than spend one night in his outpost. Security is knowing what you are doing.

One of the 'whys' I never found an answer for was that FACs were not authorized parachutes or 'Mae Wests' (flotation devices). Parachutes had limited value in low, slow flying airplanes but our mission profiles changed as anti-aircraft guns proliferated in A Shau Valley, the DMZ and Khe Sanh areas. Some places we had to maintain three thousand feet to gain any security at all. I thought parachutes should not be required but, if the pilot wanted one, he could get it. I knew I'd be very unhappy if one of my wing struts or control surfaces had been shot off and I had to sit there waiting for death while the plane fell three thousand feet.

Several times I tried to check out a few Mae Wests from Squadron Personal Equipment to use on our trips to Da Nang. If the clouds over Hai Van Pass were too low (often the case), we took the thirty-five mile water-route, over the Gulf of Tonkin, around the two mountainous peninsulas that separated us from Da Nang. An engine failure and ditching would probably be fatal without some form of flotation. The answer was always a firm NO; we weren't authorized to have them.

The emperor's airport, with only twenty-three hundred feet of runway and terrible approaches at either end, was a bit tight for the O-2 with a full combat load on a hot day. The nearest long runway was at Phu Bai and that involved driving about six miles each way on Highway One. I felt the trip would be more dangerous than the risks involved in the short field and we continued to operate out of the emperor's airport.

Good visibility for the pilot was a primary design feature in both planes. Lots of windows let in lots of sunlight. Add hot humid air to the radiantly-heated cabin and you get a steam bath. Misery was putting on a survival jacket, a flak vest, a web belt with Colt forty-five and canteen, a heavy helmet, climb into a steam bath and then go flying. Sometimes I had vision problems caused by sweat running into my eyes.

There had to be a solution. I quit wearing the flak jacket and threw the survival vest in back. That helped. One particularly hot day I gained some relief by sticking my left arm out of the window and then using my hand to hold the end of my flying suit sleeve open to the prop blast. The suit inflated like a balloon and cooler air circulated all over my body. It felt wonderful but there weren't any hands available for flying. I could hold headings and make shallow turns just using the rudder pedals and maintain altitude using elevator trim but the position was uncomfortable and I could only look down over the left side.

Janice had sent me some spring steel wire for making U-control model airplane landing gears. That night I formed a piece of it into a loop a little larger than the diameter of my sleeve. I bent the ends so that it was easy to compress into a smaller loop and place it inside the sleeve. When I let go of the ends, it expanded, forming the end of the sleeve into a funnel-shaped air scoop.

It worked. All I had to do was keep the window open and rest my left arm on the sill. Enough of the sleeve/air scoop projected into the airstream to keep my suit inflated and reasonably cool. Quality of life was raised a notch by that simple gadget.

Flying has appealed to me for several reasons: a sense of freedom, three-dimensional mobility, lots of travel, more adventure, etc. I've always been a 'rubber-necker' in the air. Shapes of clouds, meandering rivers, mountains, valleys, storms, cities – everything outside the cockpit windows interests me. VR missions in Vietnam were the same as my many pleasure flights in light planes in the States, just take off and look around. Cruising along at 85 knots and a thousand feet over Vietnam in an O-1 was scenic and visually relaxing but my thoughts were sometimes interrupted by people taking potshots at me. I could hear them very plainly, especially the sharp crack of the AK-47. Other FACs reported shots too.

I decided cheap shots were for the birds, not us. Sooner or later someone would get hit where it hurt. My favorite O-1 had fourteen bullet hole patches on its skin, so I knew they didn't always miss. I passed the word to my FACs, "If someone fires even one round at you, report ground fire and put in an airstrike immediately. If you don't know where the firing came from, just pick the most likely spot and tear it to pieces." About a month later, VR flights were as peaceful as could be and they stayed that way. No more cheap shots.

Later, as I became less enchanted with the war, I passed another bit of information to the pilots, hoping it would influence what they did in the air. "Any pilot taking great risks in action other than direct support of U.S. troops shouldn't expect any medals and he'd be in trouble with me. When U.S. troops are involved, do everything you can."

I started taking every new FAC on an indoctrination flight over the two provinces, showing him hot spots and tricks that might help him survive. Afterwards, I gave a father-son lecture about the stupidity of getting killed. There were times heroic actions were required and they took them. If anything but luck contributed to the survival record of my FACs, it was avoiding unnecessary, unjustified risks.

Night flying has advantages. The air is smoother and cooler, and there is usually less traffic. City lights are beautiful, the moon and stars are brighter when viewed from above the ground haze. Mountains and clouds look like ghosts in moonlight. Thunderstorms flicker silently in the distance. Up close, they are more exciting. At night in clouds, when conditions are right, static charges build up on the plane and you can see blue halos around the windows and giant, ten-foot sparks jump off the wingtips and nose. All kinds of interesting things can be seen better when it's dark.

One night flight was required during my P-40 flight training in World War II. I expected it to be a piece of cake because my previous night flying experiences in BT-13s and AT-6s had been fun. Both of those airplanes had radial engines with large exhaust collector rings and outlets on the sides, down low. Exhaust flames did not affect your vision. The P-40s had in-line V-12 engines with a very short exhaust stack on each cylinder. In take-off and landing attitudes, you couldn't see anything over the long nose. Instead, the pilot had to look around the engine on each side. It just so happened that the exhaust stacks were level with the horizon, where you needed to look when aligning your plane with the runway on take-off and judging your height during landing.

On take-off, flames came back past the cockpit, I wandered all over, trying to sort out runway lights from the flames. The landing was even worse because, at idle, a rich fuel mixture turned the flames from blue to yellow, the same color as the lights. Thanks to a long, wide runway, I made it without breaking anything but it taught me one thing: some planes are better than others for night flying.

O-1 cockpit lights were from the dark ages: two old fashioned World War II type ultra-violet floodlights mounted on the windshield frame. O-2s had modern post lights mounted on the panels. Exhausts on both were below the engine and flames were not visible from the cockpit. The O-2 was my choice for night flying because of the cockpit lights and two engines but we flew whatever was available.

Our airport in Hue was not a good place for night operations. The short, narrow runway, located in a densely populated area, had no beacon light, no runway lights, no approach lights and hazards at both ends. A canal crossed the south approach, about fifty feet from the end of the runway end and a pagoda towered above the trees about a block from the north end.

Nevertheless, we flew many night missions out of the field without an accident. A beacon wasn't needed because you just looked for the place where there weren't any lights in the west part of town. That was the airport. Being completely familiar with the field, it wasn't difficult to figure out about where the runway was within the dark spot. Sometimes, when a landing time was predictable, a mechanic would stand on the end of the runway, trusting soul that he was, and hold up a strobe light from one of our survival packs. We scrounged some battery-powered runway lights but the few that weren't stolen the first time we used them soon went dead and no replacement batteries were available. They were probably being sold by supply people who felt they needed the money more than we needed the batteries.

Most night flying for FACs in Vietnam was usually in the form of an airborne alert during peak tension periods, as forecasted by intelligence information. Once in a while, when an outpost had difficulty repulsing an attack, a FAC would be scrambled.

Spookys, with their side-shooting mini-guns and big parachute flares, were ideal for stopping attacks on outposts. Occasionally, on extra busy nights, Spookys weren't available and the FAC would have to make do. Illumination was essential. We usually carried two large (one million candle-power) parachute flares on night flights. Sometimes high powered illumination was all that was needed to discourage the enemy. They didn't know if Spooky was about to rain lead on them or some fighters would swoop down and sprinkle CBUs (small anti-personnel bombs) over the area.

Working Spookys was easy at night once you knew where the enemy was. When action was hot, there were usually small mortar-launched flares and machine gun tracers lighting up the place so you knew where the friendlies were. VC scattered around an outpost weren't so visible.

Quang Dien got hit hard one night while I was up on airborne alert. A Spooky that had been orbiting Da Nang was diverted. He arrived on the scene about twenty minutes after I did. My second flare was about to go out when he took over illumination (dropping flares) and asked me to mark a target. The man on the ground and I had real problems finding one. It seemed the firing was coming for all quadrants and no well-defined troop concentration was discernible. However, illumination was helping so I kept Spooky orbiting and flares coming while people on the ground tried to work out a target for his mini-guns. I was in a tight circle, down below the flares, looking for muzzle flashes when I just missed hitting a large gray thing floating in the air. It was a flare parachute!

They are big parachutes, about fourteen feet across, made out of tough nylon cloth with fifteen or twenty strong nylon cord risers. In this case it was holding a burned-out flare canister. There was no doubt in my mind that running into one of them in an O-1 would be a very unpleasant experience.

I had set up Spooky to head into the prevailing wind during his drop passes so that the flares would drift downwind in a line over the outpost. My orbit was off to one side and, I presumed, clear of the flare paths. The winds were light that night and what I hadn't realized was that the wind at my altitude, under the flares, was from almost the opposite direction. I looked around and found five or six burned out flare chutes wandering back into the target area at my altitude – big gray things ready to foul my propeller, cover my windshield, pull me into a spin.

Just about then the people on the ground spotted movements and firing in the area right under me. I marked the target for Spooky and got out of the way while he used his mini-guns. The long stream of orange tracers coming out of the black above and into the flickering flare light were right on target.

I set Spooky up on the same FM radio frequency as the man on the ground so he could adjust fire directly. After only a few more squirts of lead from Spooky, Quang Dien reported all quiet. We went into stand-by orbits to see that it stayed that way. I moved about five miles away. Burned-out flare parachutes came down very slowly. Putting a white nylon gown on my blacked-out O-1 would not be fun. Taking a black nylon gown off something warm and soft was much more appealing and I had to be careful or I wouldn't get to do it again.

Jungle ambushes by the VC killed many of our troops. They were not above trying some airplane ambushes too. I was on my way out to A Shau one day when I spotted a personnel-type parachute laying on the ground in a clearing. Could a pilot be down? Some investigation was in order. There were no beeper signals or any voice transmissions on the UHF radio guard channel. I circled at a respectable altitude and took a long look. One thing bothered me; the canopy was spread out very neatly and the risers converged on the harness almost symmetrically; something very rare in a typical parachute landing. Then another observation convinced me it would be suicide to go lower and investigate any further: the canopy was spread out upwind from the harness; something that just wouldn't happen. I felt sure there were a bunch of VC down there around that clearing with fingers on their triggers. I circled a few more times, just to tease them and then resumed my course out to A Shau. On the way back, I returned to the clearing to see if the ambush attempt was still on. It wasn't. They had rolled up their chute and gone away.

A very significant part of our good mission performance was due to excellent aircraft maintenance. Using nothing but hand tools carried in the back of their jeep and a "hip pocket" parts supply, the maintenance men accomplished everything from major engine work, such as cylinder changes, to washing the windshields.

Heat and humidity raised hell with the engines and radios. No cover, no work benches, no facilities other than two CONEX boxes and a refueling system were available to make work easier for them.

Flight schedules ran from dawn to late at night, seven days a week. It was a very hard life for the mechanics and technicians yet I didn't hear a complaint. Best of all, when they said a plane was ready, it was, every time.

Most parts and supplies came up from Da Nang, using whatever air transportation was available – helicopters, our own planes, Air America, etc. Fuel was the toughest problem. It was usually brought up by Air Force tank trucks on Highway One, which winds over infamous Hai Van pass, just a few miles north of Da Nang. Sometimes the road simply wasn't secure or a bridge had been blown up. That's when we had to find creative ways to get the required fuel. Automotive gasoline was a no-no; it had to be aviation fuel.

One time when the situation was getting desperate, a FAC volunteered that he knew some people who flew C-123s and he might be able to get one of them to fly in a load. They had big rubber bladders for carrying fuel that could be installed in the cargo compartment. Flight crews didn't like to haul them because things tended to burn rapidly if anything violent happened. I said, "Do what you can."

He got on the phone, located his buddy and described Hue in a manner to appeal to any red-blooded American who had been away from his girl very long. More specifically, he described one of the better houses and the specially attractive women in it, then guaranteed transportation to and from the house while our men pumped out the fuel. It was a deal.

Motivation is everything. The C-123 was huge compared to anything that had landed there before. Imagine shoe-horning a fuel-filled heavy transport into a 2300 foot airstrip in the middle of a large city which had poor approaches and no overruns. The runway was only slightly wider than the wheels and had no place big enough to turn around without backing up. When the plane was tucked away in our corner for the fuel transfer, one wing still projected over the runway.

It was dangerous so we never asked for C-123 delivery unless it was absolutely necessary. Also, we never missed giving the crew a ride to and from a house of desire, or any other place they wanted to go. It was a good deal. Smiles and friendly hand-shakes were always exchanged as they climbed back into their C-123. Departures were as spectacular as their arrivals and always attracted a crowd.

Chapter 10

Quality of Life

It was a dynamic war – fluid situations, high personnel turn-over, new leaders (political and military) with new plans. Only waste and killing remained constant. Most people survived but the quality of life usually left something to be desired.

Right at the bottom of the quality of life scale was living in the jungle. Leeches, rats, snakes, elephant grass, heat, humidity and rain assaulted the bodies of young men from Boston to Anchorage, loaded down with back packs and weapons. The ever-present possibility that someone had you in his gun-sights at any moment or that a booby trap was about to blow your legs off did not enhance a positive opinion of jungle living. You could add B-52 and fighter strikes to the enemy's environment. The cuisine lacked imagination. Food usually was served cold and informally. Every man sent into the jungle deserved a medal, special recognition (a jungle badge) and special pay, just like flight pay. When I talked with people down there in the jungle below me, I felt great respect for them. They were the hunters, the killers, the true sportsmen who met their opponents at the same level. No technology was there to protect them. It was wits, physical condition and luck that kept them alive.

A large step up from the jungle but still a long way from good was fire base/outpost living. Life there was largely below ground level. Heat, dust, noise (try sleeping near a frequently used cannon), mortars, enemy assaults, snipers and no privacy were prevailing detractors from quality living. Housing was temporary and tended to be informal. Materials were sandbags, steel planking, barrels, boxes and logs. Liberal quantities of barbed wire outlined more secure areas. Cuisine still lacked imagination but food was occasionally heated. I visited a few firebases during the latter part of my tour, when the

First Cav moved into the area. Overnight accommodations were not offered and I certainly didn't ask.

Life in Headquarters, like always, could be very good. Those areas were reasonably secure. Odds of getting nailed by a rocket or mortar on a large base were small. Clubs, movies, dining halls, post exchange, a few round-eyed females and an occasional air conditioner brought the overall quality to Mecca standards for those who had been out in the jungle. Yet many headquarters types failed to appreciate their environment. Details like painting rocks white, pick-up crews and even parades were part of the easy life –most often to impress visiting brass.

Top of the living scale for Americans in Vietnam was only available to a lucky few. I was one of them. A hotel suite in beautiful Hue for a year.

I shared a two room apartment on the second floor of a motel-like building. One room was about twelve by twelve feet; the other, twelve by sixteen feet. Until the Tet battle, both were cooled by ceiling fans. The bedroom contained two twin beds with comfortable foam mattresses. The bath had hot and cold running water, flush toilet and a shower. Two large clothes closets contained built-in drawers and functioned as dressers. The living room was furnished with two desks and straight chairs, two heavy rattan framed easy chairs, a coffee table and a full sized refrigerator. Hinged windows opened wide for breezes. Screens kept the flying bugs out. Three usually wholesome meals a day were served by beautiful ao dai clad young ladies in the Vietnamese-staffed, U.S. army supervised dining room. A dispensary, chapel, small theater, tennis courts and very small PX were within the guarded compound walls. From the north veranda I could see the Perfume River and Hue business district. The south veranda overlooked our tennis courts, plus schools and residences outside the compound. An ARVN jeep and driver awaited my needs six days a week. I got to drive on Sunday.

Laundry, bed-making, room cleaning were done almost automatically and at low cost by Vietnamese ladies. Food, tax-free booze and all services were cheap. Quality of life, with a few notable exceptions, was very good.

Immediately outside the compound were other goods and services highly desired by many American personnel. Top quality pot was reasonably priced. 'Ladies of the night' were available at any time. Restaurants offered food and drinks. Best of all, the city was off-limits to all American military personnel except MACV (Advisory) troops so competition for those goods and services was not intense. Prices were low and availability high.

In short, it was a good deal. However, to be completely honest, I should mention a few elements which didn't allow me, and the others, to always enjoy that high quality of living nominally available. Probably the number one detractor was a distinct lack of personal security outside and, on occasion, inside the compound. Most advisors had to go with their counterparts into the field or spend weeks in outposts. Pilots had to fly. Every morning I took off in clean clothes, freshly bathed and shaved with the scent of English Leather wafting from the open window of my little O-1. It was the only way to go to war.

Lack of security prevented me from enjoying the commercial restaurants. Four MACV helicopter pilots elected to try one of the restaurants in Hue. A hand grenade thrown into the restaurant ruined the meal. All were wounded, two critically. I ate a total of two meals in restaurants on the streets of Vietnam, hardly ever taking my eyes off the doors.

Pot, prostitutes and cheap booze could have helped pass the time but their side-effects were just too bad. There was no way I'd expose my dear wife to anything I might catch in a whorehouse. Vietnamese clap was a virulent variety, causing much pain and requiring a lot of antibiotics and faked medical records. Pot and booze might adversely affect my reactions at the time I needed them. I allowed myself only one small drink just before going to bed. Drugged fighters are just as dangerous to others as drunk drivers.

There is a very large group of people in the world who spend their entire lives in a semi-primitive agrarian environment. Peasants. They live in all sorts of shelters: caves, mud and thatch, bamboo and leaves, sheet metal and poles, stone and sod huts. China, India, Vietnam, Philippines, much of Africa, Central and South America are some of the places where they are a substantial portion of the population. Poorly educated, they have few opportunities to improve quality of life.

I saw many manifestations of the peasant/worker or privileged/non-worker system in Vietnamese people. Even the better educated people I met (ARVN officers, for example) had no concept of basic physics. It seemed as though their culture discouraged interest in physical sciences, innovation and industrial development. Perhaps it was simply that work of that type was 'beneath' the educated class, and peasants had no opportunity. For whatever reason, there was a huge void in the economic structure of the country. Industrial research, development and hard-goods manufacturing were non-existent. Machines are fundamental to increasing the standard of living.

I was concerned about their future. Making a living by tilling the soil with hoe and ox-drawn plow in this day and age means living far below our "poverty" level. Without technical knowledge, how could they hope to develop a competitive industrial or agricultural base, once peace was achieved?

I decided to try stimulating their interests in science. There simply wasn't time to teach but, with enough motivation, most anyone can learn what they want to know.

Every once in a while I'd see kids flying small kites on short strings. They weren't much – made out of scrap paper, few had frames of any kind and they didn't fly well. At least they knew that moving air could produce lift. I asked Janice to send me four or five dozen ready-to-fly hand-launched balsa wood gliders.

I taught my driver how to assemble and throw them so he could talk kids through the process. They are so impatient, I didn't want to add a language problem to their introduction to model flying. Days when spare time was available, I'd take a few gliders with me on my trips to Division and the airport. It took only one stop near a group of kids to tell me that approach wouldn't work. Most of the gliders were destroyed in seconds as they fought for possession of them, not even knowing what they were. After that I watched for single children, or groups smaller than the number of gliders I had with me. Even so, it was necessary to establish ownership and objectives before any constructive progress in assembly and flying could start.

I'll never know if any of those kids were motivated in any way towards learning more about science, but they certainly had fun with the gliders. Some showed interest in learning more so I decided to add rubber-band powered models to the program. A few older kids and adults wanted to go further, so Janice was put to work again sending kits, motors and supplies for building and flying U-control models.

Fuel for the motors was a problem. It contained alcohol and nitro-methane, definitely not mailable. Janice bought small cans, wrapped them well and placed them in the middle of big boxes so mail clerks couldn't hear the stuff sloshing around. It worked.

Later she ran into a supply problem; gliders and ready-made rubber powered models were getting hard to find in Omaha. She'd bought most of their stock. Also, costs were adding up. I tried to reduce both problems by writing the company (Paul Guillow, Inc.) that produced them, explaining in a few words what I was doing and asked if they would sell to me at wholesale prices and ship to an APO. Their response was immediate and positive. They would be pleased to help and quoted me distributor level prices.

The sales manager at Guillow thought my letter would make interesting reading and asked if he could send it to one of the model airplane magazines. Someone from Cessna Aircraft Company read about the program and they contacted me. Soon I received one hundred battery-powered plastic model Cessnas, mounted on balanced arms so they 'flew' around in circles.

The best place for flying engine-powered U-control models was on the south end of our little runway where the blacktop was wide enough for a full circle. Air America, VNAF and Army pilots cooperated. Take-offs and landings were delayed until whoever was flying U-control ran out of gas. Helicopter pilots flared and landed where down wash turbulence wouldn't cause problems.

I made my students learn how to do everything from setting up the control lines, adjusting the control surfaces and starting the engines to flying. In most cases, I gave up on their building complex models. Instructions printed in English and a zero knowledge base in related skills simply required more teaching time than I had during the days. Some nights were available but there was no suitable place for building classes. One teenager who could speak a little English showed a lot of interest and aptitude. I invited him to my room one evening for building instructions. Some people complained about his visit; how did I know he wasn't a VC? I didn't give a damn, he wanted to learn and that was the important thing.

Teaching them U-control flying was a riot. There were times all of us, spectators and flyers, were laughing so hard we could hardly stand up. I'd selected small, strong, light, trainer-type models which could take terrible crashes, usually with no more than a broken propeller. They learned by crashes. Usually, after their third or fourth crash they could manage to control the plane somewhere between straight up and straight down. Then, as success in control grew, a new aspect crept into the learning process: dizziness. Space limitations required us to fly the small planes on short lines. At top speed, the pilot had to turn completely around about every four seconds. Loss of orientation is common during the first few flights but after a little experience, it is no longer a problem.

The sound of those little, unmuffled engines turning up twelve thousand RPMs was so distinctive that a crowd gathered as soon as we started a flying session. At first crashes were humiliating, a loss of face. Everyone learned to laugh. Success, usually defined by three or more circles without hitting the ground, was glorious, with applause and cheers if the plane was on its wheels at the end of a flight. Dizzy pilots brought down the house. Some staggered and fell flat while their plane was still whirling around them. On one memorable occasion, the pilot simply let go of the control handle and the plane, dragging its control lines, took off directly towards one of our O-1s. I thought it was going to break the windshield but it missed by inches. Instead, a spectacular crash in the emperor's old, roofless hangar made everyone happy.

As skills grew, I started flying with them, two pilots with two airplanes flying in the same circle. Antics required to keep the lines from tangling were always interesting, primarily because of the language barrier. One had to guess what the other guy's plans were. The noise, frantic actions and unpredictable conclusion of every flight pleased them beyond anything I expected. Given time and supplies, it looked like hundreds could be involved. I thought it would be excellent motivation to learn more about engines, design, physics and aerodynamics.

Cessna asked for a photograph of the kids with their models so one day I lined up a few and asked someone to snap the shutter. It turned out that day was just a few days before Tet. After the battle I learned that two of the boys in the photo had been killed. Damned war! Could they have been killed by some of the sky spot bombs I'd set up?

Not long after I started buying gliders and construction kits directly from Guillow's, they sent me an interesting letter. In it, the writer explained that they were planning to produce a flying scale model kit of the O-1 and, as usual, they would make it in the configuration of one particular airplane. He asked me if I could send photographs and historical information on one of our airplanes. They would use it to produce the scale model kit.

There was no doubt which one it would be: Old 500, an O-1E, my favorite. I photographed it from every angle and researched its maintenance records. At that time, "500" had more than fifty-five hundred flying hours on it and was running on its ninth engine. The government had received a lot of service out of that cheap little O-1.

She received major damage up at Quang Tri a few weeks before I rotated. I heard that parts of her and another O-1 were to be combined to make one good airplane but I didn't learn which aircraft tail-number was used.

Guillow, true to their word, produced the kit. In appreciation for my input, they sent me the first kit off the production line. I was surprised to see the kits were still being produced and on hobby shop shelves in 1992.

My tour in Vietnam ended six weeks after Hue had been retaken. Survival and recovery were paramount interests at the time and there just weren't enough opportunities to get things going again. I gave everything left to those I thought would use them. Maybe I did some good; maybe I didn't. Anyway it was fun.

Just a few days after arriving in Hue to begin my tour, I learned the Thua Thien FACs had 'adopted' a small orphanage in the southwest part of the city. It was run by two Vietnamese nuns. They were trying to care for about forty kids with virtually no money. Facilities were minimal; some children had cots but most slept on platforms of dirt covered with thin grass mats. One classroom with one blackboard and an assortment of chairs was the extent of educational facilities. The FACs scrounged powdered milk and a variety of foods from the mess halls in Da Nang and our compound. Paper, pencils and anything else they felt the nuns could use found its way to the orphanage. When scrounging wasn't good, the pilots collected money and bought what was needed. Before Christmas, they purchased geese and other native foods for a traditional banquet.

I helped make deliveries a couple of times but soon found excuses. It wasn't the kids; I loved them. It wasn't the nuns; they were small, gentle ladies. It was the way they showed their appreciation. As in our society, it was customary to offer refreshments to guests after being invited, by sign language in this case, into their home. They didn't have much. A table, two chairs, and one wooden closet in one room. On top of the closet, inches away from a sheet metal roof, they kept two or three bottles of Vietnamese beer that I suspect were there only for us. All Americans like beer, don't they?

If you want to test your self-control, try drinking thick, bitter beer from a bottle so hot it is uncomfortable to hold and then smiling. I'd never developed a taste for beer but there was no way to escape this ritual without offending them and that was the last thing they deserved. I had nothing but admiration for those two nuns. The buildings were badly damaged during the Tet battle. Afterwards, both the nuns and kids were gone.

Individually and collectively, Americans tried very hard to improve the quality of Vietnamese life. Kindly acts were far more common than those causing pain and death.

More than a few Americans found peasant living conditions so far below their own that they tended to regard Vietnamese as subhuman. I'd seen it before in India and China during World War II. I'll never forget the officer/pilot who used Indians as targets for his slingshot, firing rocks at them. The day I saw him hit an elderly man, riding a bike, in the face and then whoop for joy was the day I snapped. Despite his higher rank, I told him where to put that goddamned slingshot. In his mind, monkeys and Indians were the same sort of animals, neither worthy of any consideration.

Some Americans were driven to acts of violence by conditions so far outside the realm of their world back home that they will never be understood by those who have not experienced the same conditions. Nothing we did there would begin to match the terrible things Vietnamese did to their own people. No matter how bad it was for us, it was worse for them.

Chapter 11

Rules of Engagement

War is not for the weak at heart. It's open season on humans, no holds barred. A contest of wits and muscle, for survival, riches, power and other less tangible goals, such as freedom and happiness.

Few people go willingly to war. People send people or get sent. Being one of those who got shot at, I resented the senders telling me when I could shoot back. After a while, I didn't let the stupid rules cloud my thinking. Weak people lie to gain a temporary advantage. In Vietnam, rules of engagement as defined by Johnson, McNamara, et al. made me weak. I lied and so did many others. It was that or greatly increase the odds of losing the battle or my life.

I signed at least a half dozen documents stating I'd read and understood the rules of engagement. The military bosses had all of the SYA (save your ass) papers they needed. No one ever questioned me on the appropriateness of any application of air power once approval had been granted. It was SYA all the way for them, not war.

Rationalizing may be simply lying to oneself. I think that's what I did. Anyway, I learned early to interpret situations to the advantage of the fighting men when applying for power from above: airstrikes.

My second week in Hue, I was over a small ground operation southwest of the city being conducted by ARVN with U.S. advisors. They started taking fire from an area up ahead of them. Just as I turned towards the area, three men ducked into a small gray building. It was about a ten-by-twenty foot brick building with a tile roof and some trim around the edges. There were a lot of tombs in that area and it could have well been one, or used to be one since the door was off. My radio contact on the ground confirmed that the fire had come from that area so I asked for air support, describing the building as possibly a tomb. Fortyfive minutes later I was still circling while my request to waive the rules probably went half-way around the world.

With the VC holed up in that building, firing stopped so the friendlies got up and walked away. They wanted the air strike to kill the VC because far less risk was involved for them. I finally said to hell with it and left. The VC walked away too.

One of the rules of engagement (for me) specified that I could not enter Laotian air space. One day an extra pair of fighters came out to A Shau, looking for a target, and I put them in on a truck park about five hundred meters inside Laos. The coordinates I gave for the target were in Vietnam. I couldn't tell the truth. Smoke and flames told me we'd destroyed a few trucks. They quit using that area for a truck park. The Laotian government didn't complain, the NVA didn't complain and the senders didn't need or didn't want to know.

As long as some people give guns to other people and tell them to use the things to enforce laws or win wars, we're going to have problems. Life or death situations provoke extreme emotions. Clear thinking and correct responses in every case is impossible.

In Vietnam, we were the strangers. We stood out. A lot of the enemy were just a part of the civilian population. You could only identify them by their actions. It doesn't take long to pull a trigger or toss a grenade. Total insecurity produced by the circumstances drove some people nuts. Good men with sincere desires to do right went psycho within weeks. Others rationalized, adapted.

Harry Longfellow told me about the time near the end of his tour when a Marine captain, new in country, rode with him on a mission. They were over a farming area in Quang Tri province, about ten miles south of the DMZ. A person, clad in black pajamas, was hoeing a field in a free-fire zone. He continued working despite the presence of the O-1. The captain yelled, "VC! VC!" and pointed. Harry just nodded; a man has a right to till his field and at least half the farmers in Quang Tri wore black pajamas. He flew on.

The captain became adamant. "That's a VC down there! What are you going to do about it?" Harry had seen a lot of killing and he just didn't believe that farmer, trying to scratch out a living in an area of scorched earth, was a big threat. What's more, he didn't feel like trying to explain the whole thing. Harry stuck his forty-five Colt pistol out the window and emptied it, aiming only to avoid shooting the airplane tire and wing strut. The captain didn't say another word during the rest of the flight. The same rules through two different pairs of eyes.

Many Vietnamese were unjustly killed and hurt. So were a lot of Americans and people from other nations. Would there be as many wars if politicians who voted or mandated war had to join the ranks? Would they establish and follow rules of engagement for themselves while the enemy had none?

Chapter 12

INTELLIGENCE?

Some books and personal accounts of the war from both sides have confirmed what we believed then: that there were many VC and communist supporters in South Vietnamese government and military forces. Some of them held high offices. The only ARVN officer I had one hundred percent confidence in was Gen. Truong. He stuck it out to the end in 1975, moving out to a ship in Da Nang harbor when the city fell to NVA troops.

I didn't condemn Vietnamese for split or changing loyalties. They had suffered through exploitative colonizations by both French and Japanese plus self-government riddled with corruption and several factions seeking to gain control by whatever means possible. Survival for the average person consisted of being on the side that won. It wasn't all that simple with family influence, religious issues, political beliefs, and personal goals affecting decisions but I felt it was the prevailing force in determining loyalty.

During the last month of my tour, when news clippings from Omaha indicated a strong swing towards U.S. withdrawal, I advised several ARVN officers to prepare for a loss of U.S. support and NVA occupation of South Vietnam. Some didn't like what I said but I was concerned about their future. I hope they are in a better place now and enjoying life.

Most Vietnamese, when captured by the other side, became cooperative – a matter of survival. I don't know if they had general orders to continue resistance when captured like we have. There were no rules followed regarding the handling of prisoners. Torture, starvation and killing were accepted practices. Life is cheap in the Far East. Welfare of another person who was in conflict with your group or simply bore the humiliation of capture, was of no consequence. In short, when captured, spill your guts and act contrite or say hello to pain then kiss the world good-bye.

If I wanted to be sure some information did not get into VC and/ or NVA hands, I had to avoid any contact with ARVN staff. Some intelligence agency mimeographed little encoding booklets that were passed to field commanders, FACs and others. It assigned code names and gave a system for encrypting grid coordinates. Thus, if the codes were actually secure, we could set up airstrikes and report intelligence information using radios without the enemy knowing what was going on. There was no doubt in my mind that the VC got their copies as soon as we did.

All FACs were assigned call signs which they retained as long as they were flying in a defined area. The Air Force FACs working in the two northern provinces had the 'Trail' prefix; mine was Trail Three Zero. Other FACs working outside of Vietnam (north of the DMZ and over Laos) had different call signs.

Probably one-third of the pre-planned airstrikes put in the northern two provinces while I was there were targets determined by intelligence acquired from captives, deserters and agents.

Some were good, some were bad. My first pre-planned, agent identified strike was located on the face of a very steep ridge, near the top, in a position where Da Nang would be in sight. The report said it was a 'rest camp.' I couldn't believe anyone would climb that steep face, get five hundred feet from the top and then make a rest camp. The place was too far from water; cover was poor with bare earth and rocks between widely scattered trees. Nuts! Some guy needed to make money or save his neck so he said what they wanted to hear.

I was so sure there was no one down there I flew close to the face and ridge top. It looked as though man had never set foot in the area. About that time, the fighters arrived. I was new and unsure so I put the flight in on the designated coordinates, making only landslides and matchsticks.

I thought about it on the way back to Hue. What a waste! After that, I adopted a policy of liberal interpretation of target coordinates developed from intelligence information. When it was highly likely that the exact coordinates or target information was inaccurate (a truck park on a cliff?), I put it in where the bombs might do more good. Even so, I'd bet that two-thirds of those pre-planned strikes were a total waste. The NVA out there probably watched us put in intelligence-based strikes saying, "Those crazy Americans have found a new bomb disposal area."

In addition to dubious intelligence, two other factors worked against all airstrikes controlled by FACs. The VC and NVA had radios and maps with coordinates too. If they heard anything from any source about an airstrike in their area, you could bet it would be deserted in minutes.

I learned about the other factor in an interesting way. One of my favorite ARVN officers was Lt. Qua who worked in intelligence. One day I requested him to do something for me: ask captured VC/NVA troops what type of aircraft-delivered ordinance they feared most. My plan was to use more of what they liked least. I expected napalm would be high on the list or, perhaps, CBU (small bomblets with air brakes that dropped slowly and exploded at ground level, spreading an awesome amount of shrapnel).

The answer came a few weeks later. It was 'those rockets that make white smoke.' Phooey! They were essentially harmless unless a person got a direct hit. I asked why. The answer was that they knew all hell would break loose as soon as there was white smoke near them. I guess intelligence was right. I'd hate to see white smoke too, under those conditions.

Thinking back, I'd been using smoke rockets for months to herd people out of areas where they shouldn't be. Their reaction to a rocket going off one hundred feet from them was always a decisive, high velocity departure in the opposite direction. Now I had a better idea of their view.

Nevertheless I kept the faith and developed a plan for intelligence-directed strikes. I'd take off about an hour and a half before on-target time and head indirectly for the area to be hit – like a FAC on a VR flight, just wandering around. As I went by, never directly over, the area, I'd evaluate the target. Any water nearby for a rest camp? Any way to get a truck there from the road? Anywhere near the many north-south trails?

After the sneak look, I'd fly around doing VR work while setting up in my mind a rendezvous point about five minutes from the target on the best approach heading and other details for working the fighters. I'd try to be within a few minutes of the rendezvous as target-time approached. When the fighters came up on my radio frequency I'd direct them to the rendezvous and head there too. briefing them on everything except the target location. By the time we met, they were briefed and ready. I'd tell them to hold their attack altitude (5,000 to 10,000 feet) and follow me, circling to compensate for my 85 knot speed. About one minute from my marking pass I'd tell the first man to get into position to follow me down. When things worked right, both of us rolling into our dives at the same time, the first ordinance would hit the target within fifteen seconds of being marked by a smoke rocket.

It was very difficult to make realistic evaluations of strikes in jungle areas. Secondary explosions and petroleum fires were rare. Sometimes we did receive reports from agents. One I remember for its detail. I had liked the target selection point. At the coordinates, there was a flat area with a medium-sized stream running along one edge. Trails were visible several miles north of the area but none at that point, primarily because of dense, high jungle. I put the strike in using my no-notice technique. About a month later, Lt. Qua handed me a translated copy of an agent's report on the strike. The target was a rest camp and they had been caught totally unprepared. Ten or twelve people had been killed. The report continued, mentioning that the dead were buried and banana trees planted on their graves to conceal them.

Some people compared the impact of the rules of engagement to fighting a war with one hand tied behind your back. The intelligence situation was similar. When fighting in a support role, coordination requirements and joint operations made it virtually impossible to achieve any significant surprise advantage. Another hand was tied behind your back.

Most FACs were not blood-thirsty harbingers of death from above even though some directives encouraged it. An area near the 'Street Without Joy', northeast of Hue, was a hot-bed of anti-government activities when I first arrived. We received occasional ground fire while VR-ing that area. I watched villagers convene in morning markets while others spread out and worked in the fields. It was interesting. Capitalism at work where communism was extolled. It was made a free-fire zone and all the people who would go were moved to new government camps. In days, the whole area became a wasteland, empty houses, empty roads, no livestock, uncultivated fields.

The author standing beside an O-2. Walls in the background are all that remains of the Emperor's hangar. A typhoon removed the roof some years back.

Hue in September, 1967. Lower arrow is over the MACV compound, pointing to the two-story building where I lived. The upper arrow points to the Emperor's airport. Air Force FACs for Thua Thien province operated from this airport.

The square area defined by a wall, starting a few blocks south of the runway was the Emperor's palace grounds. Zig-zag shaped wall and moat surrounds the Citadel area. An excellent article by Tran Van Dinh in the November 1989 issue of "National Geographic" provides a look at post-war Hue. (Robert C. Mikesh)

Hue Citadel airport in 1967. The arrow points to the area used by U.S. Air Force FACs. Three airplanes immediately below the arrow are parked in what used to be a hangar for Emperor Bao Dai's airplane until he was removed from power in 1954. A typhoon in 1959 tore the roof off. (Robert C. Mikesh)

Hue, March 2, 1968. Looking south from a point near the west wall of the Citadel. An arrow identifies the building I lived in, within the MACV compound. My short but exciting helicopter ride across the river to the 1st Division, ARVN compound, started at an LZ in the park on the river's edge, to the left of the bridge. We flew along the west edge of the canal in the lower left of the photo, runners hitting the trees, during fierce fighting with heavy artillery support.

Destruction of NVA fortifications in the Citadel wall and downtown buildings was almost one hundred percent. Many structures still standing were gutted by fires. At the time of this photo, wood planks had been tied to portions of bridge structure still above water so pedestrian traffic could be accommodated. (Robert C. Mikesh)

To help high flying fighter-bomber pilots spot low flying FACs, smoke grenades mounted on O-1 wing armament racks were ignited. Pilots pulled the ignition pins by yanking on wires extended into the cockpit at the wing root. The result was similar to sky-writing: colored smoke streamers. A steel sheet metal deflector protected the wing from defective grenade explosions and excessive heat.

FACs flying night missions usually carried two one-million candle-power parachute flares. They could light up a large area for about five minutes. Also, they usually had an incendiary log on the floor behind the front seat. It was a flare that ignited when it hit the ground and was used to mark targets. The pilot threw it out the window; a technique not far removed from World War I.

'Old 500', an O-1E and my favorite airplane. A flying scale model of it is still available in kit-form in many hobby shops. The manufacturer is Guillow's and the kit number is 902.

Handy pockets on the back of the O-1 pilot's seat held colored smoke plus a few fragmentation grenades just in case. The smoke grenades were for marking your position if forced down. Sometimes they were thrown out the window to mark targets.

The O-2 with rocket pods, wing-racks and a profusion of antennae was not the streamlined, high performance passenger airplane Cessna had set out to produce for the private market.

The office of an O-1. Strictly basic equipment. The M-16 has two magazines taped to the sling and a third taped to the bottom of the fourth, which is in the gun.

An O-1 set up for a night mission with one parachute flare and two marking rockets on each wing.

Sgt. Shanklin servicing one of our O-2s. He and his crew kept 'em flying day and night in terrible conditions; no shelters, no shops. Fuel was sometimes a major problem and keeping it from being stolen was an even greater task.

A combat-ready O-2 over South Vietnam. A different paint job, a few less windows, radios and ordnance rack and it would be a Cessna Model 337 Super Skymaster. The Air Force took delivery on 223 during 1967 and 154 in 1969. (Robert C. Mikesh)

A fan mounted on the prop shaft pulled enough air through the O-2 rear engine compartment to keep it cool on the ground. While flying, ram air taken in the above-wing duct and exhausted through adjustable doors (below arrow) provided adequate cooling. (Robert C. Mikesh)

Although never intended for combat, the Cessna 337/O-2 air frame proved it could accept significant battle damage and still fly. This one took a direct 37 mm hit and still flew back to its base at Ubon. Oil leaks due to shrapnel caused the rear engine to fail en route. (Robert C. Mikesh)

A VNAF O-1 and this USAF O-1 turned on to final approach for landing at Hue at the same time, one from a left turn, one from a right turn. This happened April 23, 1967, about three weeks before I arrived. Pilot and injuries are unknown. (Robert C. Mikesh)

Major Robert Mikesh wanted a war souvenir and got it in the form of this shrapnel-torn O-1 rudder, damaged in a mortar attack at Da Nang, January 9, 1968. Believe it or not, he took it home! (Robert C. Mikesh)

WP (white phosphorous) rockets used for marking targets. This pod is mounted on an O-2. To reduce weight, most missions were flown with less than full loads. Two pods (standard configuration) could hold 14 rockets. Sometimes one pod would be loaded with HE (high explosive) heads and one with WP. FACs occasionally used a "reconnaissance by fire" technique, shooting rockets into suspect areas to see what happened. (Robert C. Mikesh)

Pilfering was a problem in Vietnam as it is anywhere in the Far East. All compound employees had to undergo a routine search on their way out. Gifts had to be accompanied by a note to the guard to get them out of the gate. This is quitting time at the MACV compound in Hue. (Robert C. Mikesh)

End of a day in Hue. Jeeps coming in from outposts and offices. compound employees walking home. That's Vang behind the Jeep. (Robert C. Mikesh)

In the 'Street Without Joy' area during a Division operation. I didn't feel very useful on the ground and was rarely needed. One FAC in the air was better than two on the ground.

We were told that anyone sighted in that area was to be considered enemy and take appropriate action. I hated that phrase 'appropriate action.' What they really said was, "Do what you want to do until you get into trouble then whatever you did wasn't what you were authorized to do." More bullshit from above.

Long talks with my FACs showed general agreement that most people we found during the day in those free-fire areas on the coastal plains were frustrated farmers, people living on the edge of those zones taking risks to glean fields, streams and buildings.

I found a child attending a water buffalo, grazing in a field about one mile inside the free-fire zone. I herded both of them back to safety with smoke rockets. It was simple, just put the rocket on the side you want them to go away from.

One day I found a sampan load of people going up a narrow canal near the middle of a free-fire zone. It looked like a mixture of men, women and children. Were some VC and others hostages? Why, if the movement was hostile, would they risk traveling in daylight when there were no outposts or government troops within several miles of that area? Travel at night would be relatively secure.

I came down lower and took a good look. No children but some appeared to be young women. They continued to paddle up the narrow canal despite my obvious presence. They appeared concerned, watching me closely, but didn't change their course.

Talk about being judge and jury! I sat there in my O-1 with full authority, impunity, to determine continuance of their peaceful (for the moment) lives, the stark terror of an airstrike, injuries and pain, possibly death. I decided to compromise; scare the hell out of them.

Since my rockets never hit exactly where I thought they would, I aimed the plane directly at the sampan, figuring the safest place was right there. It was one of my more accurate rockets, hitting the canal bank right opposite the center of the boat.

What a reaction! It looked as if the sampan exploded but it hadn't been touched. In seconds it was floating along by itself, with only froth and waves that looked more like motorboat wakes, to testify that people were in the area. They disappeared in low growth along the canal. I didn't see one move as long as I stayed in the area.

In the eyes of some, I may have flunked my judge and jury test but at least I could live with myself. That's something we all have to do.

Most of the coastal free-fire-zone areas were within artillery range of various ARVN and RF batteries. They had some good gunners; plenty of practice. If people ducked into a hut or hid from me as I approached and it was a slow day, I'd radio the U.S. advisor at the nearest outpost with artillery, tell him what I had for a target and ask if they wanted a fire mission. They'd check with their counterparts and, if the Vietnamese thought VC were active in that area, it would be a go. I'd give the coordinates in the clear (no encryption; it took too long) and, in a minute or two, a round would be on its way. One time, they dropped a round right through the roof of a building I'd seen a person duck into. Beautiful shooting. Usually they inflicted major damage on the target within a few shots.

Chapter 13

Macho Men, Bravery and Ego

Why do so many men spend so much money and effort to shoot deer and ducks or hook a fish? Why do some men like war? An answer began to form after I read about the results of a study. It concerned human identical twins separated at birth and raised in different environments. Researchers found that objectives, selections and motivations were remarkably similar even though they were raised in dissimilar environments. The conclusion was that heredity shaped human character more than most people had thought.

For most of the two million or so years that life in human forms has trod on this earth, they have survived by being good hunters and foragers, working cooperatively in groups. At least, that's what most archaeologists hypothesize, based on their studies of primitive sites.

Surely, in two million years, the successful behavior pattern of cooperative hunting has been deeply engraved in genetic codes. Coupled with that, I believe, is an inborn need for individuals to feel useful to others, be it another person, family, friends, team or society. Like all other traits, there are substantial variations between individuals in relative strengths of those drives.

Other recent studies substantiate the idea that there are differences in the way men and women think. I attribute this also to genetic codes. Males probably did most hunting, taking the higher risk jobs in successful groups because one male can service many females. If a group lost most of its men, it could recover in numbers fairly fast. Not so, the other way around.

There is another personality trait I attribute to genetic codes. Males must be driven to accept risks typical with hunting and travel. It is done by giving them frail egos, the kind that require frequent reassurance that they are indeed successful males, fulfilling the societal image they believe to be important.

Some incidents I observed in Vietnam but didn't always understand, in view of these later studies and some thought, now appear to me to be normal manifestations of genetically instilled behavior.

One personality trait I have never appreciated is the male 'blowhard.' You see and hear them in "show and tell" sessions, convincing themselves and others how great they are; maybe that's why men write books about war. During the fifty years since my first date with a girl, I have joined only two predominately male social groups, one model airplane club and one ultra-light airplane club. In both cases, I evaded most social functions, participating primarily in flying activities. During my many years of private flying, I avoided spending any extra time in airport offices. That's where the guys wearing baseball caps with scrambled eggs on their visors hang out, waiting for an audience.

There was a higher ranking army officer in the MACV compound at Hue for a while; I'll call him Jake. He had a large, constantly inflated chest and walked with a swagger similar to a linebacker who has just sacked the other team's quarterback. Jake's 'conversations' largely concerned how great, how brave he was. Phrases like, "I got me a gook today" seemed to predominate.

About noon on the second day of the Tet attack, a few of us were sitting outside the command post trying to figure out what was happening and what to do. Someone asked if anyone had seen Jake. We looked at each other – no one had seen him since the attack. He'd been in the Officers' Club late the night before. The thought hit us, maybe Jake got zapped during the initial attack. He lived in a room by himself and could be lying there wounded or dead.

One of the army men went to check his room. He came back a few minutes later with a disgusted look on his face. Jake was in his room, under his bed, where he had been for the last day and a half. Beneath that veneer of macho swagger, Jake was chicken.

Another army officer, a first lieutenant, was just the other way around. His job was advisor for an ARVN outpost and he stayed there most of the time. When visiting the compound for supplies and a little R and R, he read a lot and stayed away from the club – a quiet, introspective person. During the big battle he was all over the place, helping in calm, constructive ways. During a furious firefight right in front of the compound on the second day, when the Marines were trying to get out of the gate, I saw him run out into the street where bullets were whizzing everywhere and help the Marines drag their wounded and dead back. My rationalization for not being out there with him was that I happened to be upstairs in the main building at the time. I'm no hero, never have been, never will be.

What makes the difference? I decided it was compensation. Men who are not confident of their manliness role create a shell of words, thoughts and behavioral patterns to bolster their self esteem. Those who are confident in their role don't worry about appearances.

To this day, I don't trust men in terse situations (business, sailing, flying, etc.) who show strong tendencies to cultivate a macho image. Owning a four-wheel drive pick-up with oversize tires, light bars and gun racks that has never been off paved roads is an example.

Surviving and winning a pitch battle produces real emotional highs in most men.

One evening after dinner, most of the pilots, including me, were in the Thua Thien ALO's room, going over the day's activities and planning tomorrow's as we usually did in a very informal way. Capt. Bosworth had run into some extra action coming back from his late afternoon VR mission. It was dark when he came in, his eyes bright and sparkling. He was so excited and pleased he couldn't sit down. We heard his story.

A Marine patrol was moving into a night defensive position (NDP) on a hill about fifteen miles northwest of Hue when they were attacked. The FAC just happened to be in the area and heard their call for help. It was a good thing. The radio operator told him they had not been able to raise any ground stations. He called for fighters and helicopters, tore up the area around the patrol and got them extracted just before dark. Despite intense ground fire reported by the patrol, there were no casualties. He was pleased, as he should be, and I'm sure that encounter is regarded by him as a great memory.

Every man sent out on jungle patrol should get a medal just for surviving in such a miserable environment. I thought I could take it if I had to but, if I didn't, I wouldn't. Night-time in jungle is bad enough. Nighttime in a jungle with other people who have guns too, and they want to kill you, must be something very few people would look forward to.

Late one afternoon I was coming back to Hue from the north end of A Shau Valley. Just as I approached the last ridge, a little north of the Song Bo River, a Marine patrol contacted me. They were on top of a lower cone-shaped hill about one mile beyond the ridge and said they needed help. I was over them in about two minutes. I could hear ground fire and see explosions down one side of the peak. They reported being completely surrounded and taking mortar, rocket and gunfire. I called for fighters and helicopters. The wait was longer than average, about thirty minutes. During that time I circled, looking for targets and planning the withdrawal. Something bothered me; I could see the Marines on top, even watched them throw grenades down the slope. The one thing I never saw was any explosions on the top where they were. It looked as quiet as a Sunday afternoon in a small town. Even as they reported incoming and being pinned down, I couldn't see any smoke, dust or other evidence of violence. I could hear rifle fire and what was probably grenades.

Regardless of my suspicions, I had to get them out. The fighters came; we made lots of noise tearing up the area, the helicopters came and the Marines left. That action came to mind many times as I flew over the peak later on. You can't blame them for wanting out. It wasn't at all like sitting in a duckblind, anywhere in Vietnam. Those 'ducks' shot back and were just as smart as the hunters. Wherever our hunter, risk-taker, macho drives and ego needs come from, they were filled to capacity, and then some, in Vietnam.

A total lack of security in Vietnam, so different from almost total security in the States, affected people in widely different ways. Some used drink and other drugs to escape reality. Others loved it and sought more. For me, it made life simpler. Like the rabbit that lives under the bushes in our front yard, my primary goal was survival. Proof of success was the fact that I was still breathing. Thanks to Janice's competent management of the family and home, plus not burdening me with her problems, I had no worries beyond the next day. I slept better in Vietnam, with the possibility of a rocket coming in my window at any time, than I ever had at home.

A social phenomenon common to combat is fast forming friendships based on mutual trust of another's actions in life or death situations. FACs, working as individuals in virtually all combat situations, did not have opportunities to be involved in team efforts as fighter pilots did. We were loners, spread thinly over large areas.

Friendships developed from association on the ground but situations where one's life depended on another's support just didn't happen very often.

You could see the application of industrial motivation techniques in the way medals were handed out in Vietnam. It was difficult to serve a tour without getting a bunch of medals. The last thing I wanted to do was motivate someone into a posthumous award, so my standards for nominations were very high. I suspect a few of my pilots still feel they did not receive adequate official recognition.

Someone decided a FAC should get an Air Medal for every twenty missions flown. Someone else at Squadron or Group level made up a form every FAC had to fill out after each flight. Below the heading where the FAC entered his name and outfit were twenty lines for entering the date and time of each flight. When all twenty lines were filled, the form was sent into the Squadron and an Air Medal was eventually awarded to the pilot.

At the typical flying rate, a FAC was awarded an Air Medal every two weeks. When medals are passed out in such profusion, their award becomes meaningless. I felt it was like giving someone a trophy for getting out of bed.

Directing us to fill out forms and send them in upset me for two reasons. First, it reduced the significance of the medal to a premium offer – fill out this coupon and send it in for your free gift. Secondly, all the information required to award Air Medals was already available in the Squadron. Aircraft forms contained the pilot's name, serial number, date, flight time and type of mission for every flight. There was no reason Air Medal awards couldn't be made based on standard aircraft flight records.

I refused to fill out the forms. Just about every time I went into the Squadron Headquarters down in Da Nang, someone would tell me I was delinquent in Air Medal form submissions. After receiving several calls in Hue on the same subject, I sent the Squadron a letter stating that I did not desire to receive any Air Medals. That got the pressure off until my tour was finished.

Squadron regime had changed about two months before I left but nothing came up on the subject until I processed out on my way back home. The clerk looked through my records and said, "There's something wrong, Sir. There's no record of your Air Medal awards." I said I didn't want any. He wouldn't accept my answer and called the Squadron Adjutant into our discussion. He said a clerk would help me go through my "Form 5" (permanent Air Force records on all flights by a pilot) and fill out the forms. Once again I stated in a very positive way that I didn't want the goddamned Air Medals and they couldn't make me take them.

The Adjutant left for a discussion with the commander. He came back and gave the clerk authority to clear me from the Squadron without the Air Medal forms.

I'd like to say that was the end of the story but it wasn't. About two months later, at home and retired, I started getting Air Medals in the mail, both certificates and hardware. They continued trickling in for several months. I felt sorry for the clerk assigned to fill out the forms. Avoiding work wasn't my objective.

Chapter 14

Harry Longfellow

Squadron Personnel called sometime in November to let me know my Quang Tri ALO (the man in charge of the FAC detachment in Quang Tri) was going to be replaced. I was very pleased to learn the new man was Harry Longfellow. During our pre-Vietnam training I found that we didn't think the same about much of anything but I always appreciated his candor. He wouldn't be a 'yes man.'

When asked where Harry had been the last six months, the caller became evasive; said he'd been involved in a special project. I learned he was currently at Khe Sanh and would move directly to Quang Tri. Since he would still be in the same squadron, no processing down at Da Nang was necessary.

Harry and I got together a few days later so I could check him out in his new job. I wanted to find out what he'd been doing at Khe Sanh. I'd flown over the place many times and couldn't remember seeing an O-1 on the ground and wasn't aware at that time of any FAC activities in Laos. It took a while to get him talking. Even then, the only information I could get out of him concerned the living conditions at Khe Sanh – not a word about his missions.

Harry had been living at Khe Sanh most of the past six months. By process of correlating facts and voids in information I decided his group of FACs were supporting Laotian troops holding territory between the Vietnam border and Ho Chi Minh Trails. I learned later that they also worked over the roads, a very hazardous job, considering the awesome anti-aircraft gun batteries used by NVA to discourage air strikes.

The more I thought about Harry's mission, the more concerned I became over our government's hypocrisy. Secrets are secret only until it is expedient to tell others. Surely, North Vietnam had told everyone it wanted to about our presence in Laos. Surely, within diplomatic circles, it was well-known we were operating in Laos. Just why was it necessary to withhold the information from the American public and even our own military forces operating right up to the border? Was the lie (no military actions in Laos or Cambodia) justified by the possibility that admission of our involvement would make an unpopular war even more unpopular? I didn't like the implication.

He did fill me in on his living conditions for the past six months. Rocket, mortar and artillery activity was so great around Khe Sanh that airplanes parked on a ramp didn't last long. It was too far from any more secure base to give them adequate range over their assigned area in Laos. The only choice was to park the O-1s in covered bunkers. Tight little hangars were dug part way into the ground, with sides and tops built up from heavy timbers, dirt and sandbags. Ramps allowed the planes to be wheeled in and, with some effort, out of the bunkers. Protected as they were, a shell would have to hit just right to damage a plane. That's why I hadn't seen any O-1s up there. They were underground when not flying.

Harry and I went into Khe Sanh so he could show me around the place and see some of his buddies. God, what a dump! The FACs lived in crowded underground bunkers, slept in double bunks, traveled between bunkers in slit trenches and spent almost all the time they were not flying, underground. When it rained, the trenches and bunkers became cold, muddy lakes. I felt a little guilty and thankful at the same time when I thought about how nice it was in Hue, only fifty miles away.

Harry had a wife and kids back home. In all our talks and travels together, before and during Vietnam, he never made a comment or took an action that suggested anything besides complete marital fidelity. I have an inherent distrust of men who two-time their wives. If they can lie to their wives, they'll lie to you. He was one I felt I could trust.

There was one aspect of Harry's behavior that didn't correlate with his basic personality. In the air, he loved to fly dangerously. Not stupid acts like flying back and forth in heavy anti-aircraft fire but doing things with airplanes that usually aren't done.

There was a highway bridge across the Quang Tri River, just north of town. It was a very sturdy steel bridge with several spans set on concrete pilings. It wasn't a high bridge, essentially level with the banks on both sides. Harry told me he flew under it. I couldn't believe him but he was no B.S. artist.

He must have done it. Later, he told me he had flown under it many times. The reason was he liked to look up and see the expressions on peoples' faces just as he passed below them. It was a nice way to finish off a mission.

I came down low one day and looked at the bridge. There was no way I'd try sticking an O-1 under it. No way.

Harry called me one day, about two weeks before we finished our tours. He was apologetic. The conversation went something like this:

"Brownie, I just broke your favorite airplane, Old 500."

"Were you hurt?"

"No, but 500 doesn't look so good."

"How bad?"

"Well, the left gear is broken off, the left wingtip is bent, the prop's beat up. It's not in very good shape."

"When did it happen?"

"Actually, it happened about two hours ago but I had a hell of a time getting out of the plane."

"Why?"

"Well, I was landing at Quang Tri and I went off the runway and skidded into that big mine field on the east side of the runway. I had to sit there for an hour before they could get someone who knew where the mines were."

"That must have been exciting."

"Well, it was when I was going in. I don't know how in the hell I missed them. I was right in the middle when I stopped. The walk out was no fun, even with a guide."

I knew I wasn't getting the whole story. Harry was a good pilot; there wasn't a chance he'd simply lost control on landing and ground looped off the runway. I said, "We'll have to get a helicopter to airlift it back to Da Nang. Have you called them yet?"

"No, I wanted to get it straightened out with you first."

"Get what straightened out? What happened?"

"Well, you're going to hear about it sooner or later so I might as well tell you now. I was making a low pass over the compound (read that as buzzing the Quang Tri MACV area) and hit one of their big antennas with the left gear. I knew it was bent but thought it might hold together for one landing."

I couldn't get mad at Harry for telling me the truth. Instead it caused a strong feeling of empathy. Back during World War II, I had been in the same situation. The two P-47 squadrons in China had BT-13s for maintaining instrument flying proficiency but they were almost never used for that. Instead, scheduled instrument practice flights were usually used as opportunities for aerobatics, buzzing and just raising hell in general. Two pilots in the other squadron (the 92nd) had been killed the day before I was scheduled to fly. They had flown into a box canyon and couldn't climb out or turn around; an old story. Our C.O. announced there would be absolutely no more low flying in our BT-13. That afternoon I landed with three hundred feet of telephone wire trailing out behind my left wing and a damaged leading edge. He grounded me for thirty days. That hurt.

I had my approved retirement papers so they couldn't hurt my career but Harry had a ways to go. He didn't deserve to be punished but the group was short on planes and might want to make him an example.

Harry was patient; I was thinking. I asked, "Do you think the MACV guys will complain to the squadron about your buzzing?"

"No, they like it. Besides, they had an extra antenna. It's probably up by now."

"Harry, it's got to be battle damage. Then it's no sweat. How about a bullet gave you a flat tire and that caused the ground loop?"

I asked him to call Da Nang and report it direct. The fewer liars, the less chance for conflicting stories. Someone from the Squadron called me and asked what I knew about Harry's crash. My reply was that things had been really hot around the DMZ the last few days and I was happy to see him in one piece, and that was the truth.

The last night we were in Vietnam, Harry and I ate together at the Da Nang Officers Open Mess (DOOM) club. As usual, the menu listed some sandwiches, hamburger steak or the 'special of the day.' We ordered the special: fried chicken. The place was crowded. A young Air Force lieutenant, a bright and shining ground-pounder, walked up and asked if we would share our table. We invited him to have a seat. He began to study the mini-menu. After a long time, he looked up and asked, "What are we having tonight?" We both replied, "Chicken."

You could almost see the gears grinding under his short haircut. He looked up and suggested, "Perhaps we could share a bottle of wine. Colonel, what wine do you prefer with chicken?"

Something snapped inside me. Perhaps it was the idea that wine could help the god-forsaken greasy, half-cooked chicken I knew we were going to get. Perhaps it was his ingratiating manners. Perhaps I was just pissed off. I said, "Personally, with chicken, I prefer Pepsi-Cola."

Next morning, after the 707 had rotated and its wheels made their last thump on the beat-up runway, everyone cheered. I watched the green hills and blue water quickly fade to gray as we entered clouds. It would be good to get back to the world and my family but, having survived Vietnam, I was glad I got to go. It was one hell of an adventure.

Chapter 15

VIETNAM, 1988

One of my goals for many years was to visit China again and see what communism had done for the Chinese people. Chiang Kaishek was regarded by most Americans in China during the war as a corrupt, despotic leader. The term most commonly used when referring to him was 'Chancre Jack.' What most of us didn't understand back then was that the Chinese people had been governed more or less that way for tens of centuries. Feudal warlords seldom considered individual rights. Had communism improved quality of life for the peasants?

In the spring of 1980, Janice and I booked a tour of China that included many of the places I had been during World War II. The most obvious change in the people was their regard for other people's property. During the war, anything that wasn't tied down and guarded was stolen. If the guards were Chinese, we could be sure it wouldn't be there long. During our visit in 1980, they were scrupulous, accounting for every transaction with little receipts and returning anything forgotten. One of our traveling companions left a camera bag containing a lot of equipment and $9,000 in travelers' checks along side the road when we stopped a few minutes to take pictures on the way to an airport. The bag was found, turned in to the police and brought to the airport about thirty minutes later.

What had not changed was distribution of wealth. The war lords were gone. Still, the only people living above peasant level were Communist officials and, most significantly, the Politburo members and their families. They had their limos and special privileges. Their children were assured college educations and good jobs. The peasants were living in caves, huts and dormitories, still tilling their – no, the government's – fields with oxen and wooden plows.

I felt sorry for the Chinese people; they had been 'ripped off' again. Only the titles had been changed. Even worse, they had lost their strong family ties from before and seeds of distrust governed their daily actions and thoughts. I saw the Chinese brand of communism as espousing equality for all on the surface but, under a thin coat of paint, it was a graft-ridden totalitarian state.

I returned to central China on a business trip in 1987 and found considerable economic gains had been made. A few reforms had enhanced individual's choices to some extent. There was much more enthusiasm in the people and vigor in the economy. Today I see China as a group of one billion intelligent, hard-working people, hungry for knowledge and opportunity but terribly handicapped by their government.

My feelings about Vietnam were much the same, even during the war. As I expressed in my tapes and correspondence then, I wanted to return when it was peaceful and get to know the people and the country much better. Local travel agents in 1987 and again in early 1988 failed to set up a trip for me. Finally, I took it upon myself to answer a small advertisement for Vietnam travel that appeared in a military magazine. Ultimately, that approach was successful in getting me started on the trip but the execution left a lot to be desired.

The basic idea was to go to Bangkok, enjoy the sights for a few days while a travel agent there handled the process for getting a visa and booking you on your choice of three standard Vietnam government-conducted tours. They recommended a three-day rest in Bangkok before flying back home. That sounded like a good plan and it wasn't very expensive. Our younger son, Tracy, decided to go with me.

We arrived in Bangkok about two o'clock in the morning. No one met us as per itinerary. However, we knew the name of the hotel we were to stay in so we grabbed a cab. It was a long ride. The hotel clerk said they didn't have any reservations for us but a room was available. That morning, I called the Bangkok travel agency assigned to handle our trip to Vietnam. They had not heard of us. So far, all we had received for our money was a bunch of vouchers. It appeared now they might be of questionable value.

The Bangkok agent was concerned about satisfying our needs and arrived at the hotel a short time later. He looked at the vouchers, explained that our U.S. agent had contacted him several months back but no formal agreement had been reached regarding their business relationship. Despite the fact we had purchased the 'tour' about two months in advance, he had not received the money and wasn't sure he could ever get it. He put on a resigned face and said that, nevertheless, he'd honor the vouchers and start to work getting our visas and tour booked. It was interesting to learn that approval for the visas had to come from Moscow. He did his job. Three days later, we were heading for Saigon in an Air France 747. Lunch was something else: linen, silver, wines, gourmet food. Back in the bowels of the coach section, we expected a cardboard box lunch.

The lady sitting next to me was from England. She had been in Vietnam several times before as part of a team of financial experts working to set up a stronger commercial banking system. Its purpose was to attract foreign investments. Among other things, I learned from her that the Vietnam government had established a bank some time before for that purpose but its total capital assets were only $25,000, a pathetic amount that brought only ridicule, not investments.

Tan Son Nhut was deserted. A few small Russian turbo-prop transports were parked far away from the terminal in what appeared to be a storage area. Other than our airplane, nothing was moving except some boys playing on a taxi strip near the end of the runway. Growth between the paved areas was head-high.

Our guide and driver were waiting for us. We learned that the tour group consisted of two people: us. The guide's English was good and we talked during our ride to the hotel. He was an ex-English-language-school teacher. One of his first comments was that, since we were Caucasians traveling in Vietnam, the Vietnamese people would assume we were Russians. Quite a few of them were there on official business and vacations. Later we had several experiences where it was comforting to know we were probably identified as Russians.

The river was just two blocks from our high-rise hotel and we had two hours to kill before the afternoon sightseeing tour began so we took a walk down to the waterfront. Traffic was one tenth of what it had been during the war. Ninety percent of it was pedestrians and bicycles. The war-time traffic din was gone.

Stores we passed had modest inventories; not bare shelves and not over-stocked. Little had changed at sidewalk level; boys hounded us, offering anything they could find at what I would assume were ridiculous prices. We stopped at the waterfront to view river traffic.

A man approached me and offered, via sign language and a few words, to exchange money at 4,000 dong per dollar rate. That was considerably better than the 3,000 rate the guide said I could get in most shops. We bargained a little and came to an agreement for $20.00 at 5,000 to one. It involved more money than he had on him at the time so he took off, indicating he'd be back shortly. Tracy became nervous about my black market activity but I felt confident that no one would bother me for such a small transaction.

When it came to physical size, it wasn't a small transaction. Even in large denominations, 100,000 dong made a wad of bills that would choke a horse. He made a great show of counting out the money. I watched closely for any slight of hand and saw none. I pulled out my twenty dollar bill but he didn't take it at first. Instead he held out a rubber band and motioned the wad should be kept small and placed deeply in my pocket. Then he stuck my twenty in his pocket, took the stack of dong out of my hand and, in plain sight, started to roll it up tightly. About then another Vietnamese ran into me from behind. I turned around to see what the hell was going on. That's all it took. When I returned my attention to the bill-rolling job, the rubber band was in place and he handed me the roll, smiling. I had an idea I should demand a re-count but he had my twenty dollars and it probably would involve some unpleasantness. Since I wasn't on firm legal grounds, I waited until I was back at the hotel room before I unrolled it. There was one large bill on the outside and the balance were small denominations. He made an $18.00 profit on the deal. No wonder he was smiling.

Needless to say, I didn't report that episode to the police but another incident that occurred a few minutes later was brought to their attention. On the way back to the hotel, a group of boys started giving us a hard sell on street maps of Saigon. One of them held onto my left arm as though he wanted my attention while another waved the map in my face. I decided to cross the street; maybe they would get brushed off by the heavy bicycle traffic. It worked. At least I thought that was the reason they went away. Just as we stepped up on the curb, I thought I'd better check the time. Ugh! No watch. It was one of those $10 digitals I'd worn for years so the loss was only an inconvenience. I looked across the street but the kids were long gone.

Getting ripped off twice in a few minutes made me feel a little stupid but thankful I'd anticipated some plundering and had all my more valuable possessions in a money belt. Our guide was waiting when we arrived at the hotel so I mentioned the stolen watch. He took the theft very seriously, called the police and secured descriptions of the boys.

We headed for the 'Governor's Mansion' (now named the 'Reunification Hall'), a palace-like structure built during Diem's regime. A group of people were setting up several large signs, a sound system and podium on the front steps. I asked the guide what was going to take place there. It was to be a ceremony recognizing contributions of women who had supported the VC during the war. My next question was why they had waited so long – thirteen years. His answer was to the effect that ceremonies similar to this, recognizing war-time deeds, were very common and happened on a continuing basis.

We were escorted to a large conference room and requested to have a seat in the front row. After a few minutes, a well-dressed young lady came in and proceeded to give us a canned lecture in English. A major portion concerned the terrible war crimes committed by the American invaders and their ultimate defeat in 1975. It was straight party-line B.S. all the way. She may have believed it. I didn't argue but decided to show a complete lack of interest in her statements by looking out the window, checking the place on my wrist where I used to have a watch, whispering to Tracy and so on. She became a little upset and raised her voice to just a few decibels less than screaming. When she finished her diatribe, I smiled and said, "Thank you." She stomped out. We didn't learn much there.

After that, we were taken to a 'war museum.' Our guide dutifully escorted us through the exhibits, explaining them and translating signs when we asked. I felt the 'museum' should have been identified as a propaganda center. The exhibits were very pointedly arranged to show the NVA as liberators with rare mention of VC support. Without exception, the Americans were presented as invaders, guilty of heinous crimes and ultimately defeated in 1975. No mention was made of the Republic of South Vietnam, the ARVN, or any other nation's involvement. According to their history, it was American forces that were defeated in 1975.

I thought the communist propagandists were stupid to think the people in Saigon would swallow that line. Then it hit me as we passed several student groups between about seven and twelve years of age. Their teachers were lecturing earnestly. I realized those kids wouldn't hear anything but what the party wanted them to hear. Of course, what need is there for them to know the truth on any subject if they are not involved in any decisions bearing on their government?

That afternoon we went out to visit the tunnels of Cu Chi. They had constructed a pavilion complete with an area map on the front wall of an auditorium and chairs for about one hundred people. Our guide introduced us to the two attendants and explained that they had been awarded their positions in appreciation for their heroic actions against the American forces while members of the Viet Cong. No mention was made of their actions against Vietnamese citizens with different political sympathies.

Both wore stern expressions and looked us directly in the eyes often as they lectured in Vietnamese. We asked some questions to show concern about living conditions for them and their families during the war. Afterwards, their behavior was more relaxed and a few smiles crossed their faces. I suspect some were the results of inside jokes at our expense, but I didn't mind at all. After all, they had been good fighters, tough and resourceful in the face of a huge, well-equipped force. Through our guide, I told them we were very much aware of their sacrifices and admired their fighting ability, then added that it would have been much better if we had been fighting on the same side.

Somehow, that comment, as relayed by our interpreter, struck a nerve in both of them. They came up to us and shook hands. Their grips were very strong but the smiles and feelings of mutual respect were worth the pain.

Our guide asked if we would like to tour one of the tunnels. We walked about five hundred feet to an inconspicuous opening in the ground. One of the former VCs produced a flashlight and started down short steps into an underground chamber. I followed, then Tracy. A tunnel entrance was at the far end of the room. Our leader bent over and walked into it without breaking his stride. I'm just under six feet tall and Tracy is a little over. The tunnel was too low for anything but a duck walk and too narrow in some places for that so it was mostly hands and knees for us. While we were trying various means for making progress in such cramped quarters, our leader took off with the only light. I yelled for him to slow down but he didn't understand my English and I didn't know his word for 'slow.'

At one point Tracy said he couldn't take it any more and had to go back. I could hear the beginning of panic in his voice. There was no way he could turn around so my advice was to relax and keep moving, that the quickest way out should be ahead. About that time, I came to a corner and could see a little light up ahead. That information cheered Tracy and we made it to the ladder without further problems other than leg cramps and sweat running into our eyes.

We emerged wringing wet after what was probably only ten or fifteen minutes below ground. All four men were standing around the little hole we came up through, smiling and laughing. It was just possible we had been talked into a 'snipe hunt' and the joke was on us. We laughed too. It was fun, wasn't it?

We walked back to the car together and shook hands again with respect and some warm feelings for each other.

Our return route included a trip around the huge deserted army base near Cu Chi on a road built by Americans. Our guide said the best roads in Vietnam were those built by us. The mood was much more relaxed and we started to talk frankly about both the U.S. and Vietnam. We were thirsty after our tunnel crawl and I suggested we stop at one of the roadside stands and drink something. He selected one that had a little porch with chairs in the shade.

We sat there and talked for about an hour. I noticed the proprietress was cooking something that looked like mini-drum sticks. They were made of ground and seasoned shrimp molded over sticks of sugar cane and then deep fried. They were delicious and went well with our soft drinks. I felt relaxed and comfortable. I had met some of the former enemy and been able to express directly to them my admiration for their fighting ability as I had in my tapes and correspondence many times during the war. And it was true, I'd much rather have had them on our side.

The tragic end to the whole bloody affair for the VC was that, after all their sacrifices, they were not given the voice in government that they had been promised by North Vietnam. Recognition, ceremonies, jobs, yes; authority, no.

Next day we headed for Da Nang in a DC-9-sized Russian jet flown by Vietnamese. The landing was beautiful, smooth as glass.

Our new guide was older, about 40, and his grasp of English wasn't very good. We did learn that he was a combat troop in the VC and had been wounded several times. He had the scars to prove it. Like our Cu Chi guides, his job had been awarded in recognition for his part in the war.

I was looking forward to the trip up Highway One over Hi Van Pass to Hue. The road was very narrow and much rougher than I expected. It took all afternoon, even though the actual distance was only about fifty miles. Stops and slow-downs for villages, pedestrians, ox carts, a few busses and trucks kept our average speed down to about fifteen miles an hour. The Japanese-made car was old and its shocks were completely gone. It weaved and hopped all over the road despite the best efforts of our driver.

Peasants were using Highway One for rice harvesting, everything being done by hand. It was cut and shocked, carried to the road, threshed (by holding each shock against a nail-studded drum turned by hand or foot power), cleaned (winnowed), spread to dry, swept up and bagged. The process was probably unchanged from what they were doing one thousand years ago.

It was apparent Hue had seen better days. Gray mold was the prevailing color for most buildings. Except in the Imperial Palace area, most battle-damaged buildings had been repaired or torn down. The brass cannons, formerly positioned under tall, heavily timbered, tile-roofed structures, had been relegated to low sheet metal roofed sheds. Only temporary repairs were apparent within the Palace walls, such as propping up sagging roofs.

Our contacts with others in Hue were friendly, even those we met walking around. A few students practiced their Russian by greeting us with "Dos bidiania" as we passed. The MACV compound had been converted to some sort of government building. Tracy and I wanted to walk inside and look around but the unfriendly stare we received from a man standing on the balcony near my old room discouraged us. Perhaps he, too, thought we were Russian.

Next morning we traveled by boat up the Perfume River to a large pagoda at the west end of town. Our car met us there and, as we headed towards town, I asked the guide if it would be possible to visit a huge tomb located south of town that I had flown over and admired many times during the war. I remembered it as an area of ten to twenty acres surrounded by a high gray brick wall, with a lake, four or five buildings and wide walks inside. There was some discussion between the tour guide, our Hue guide and the driver. Finally, the answer was yes. The place I described was Emperor Tuduc's tomb.

It was more beautiful than I had expected. The setting was ideal for a person who sought a quiet, secure, restful, orderly retreat. Rampant foliage was held back by wide brick walks and embankments. Walks and steps led us past lake-side fishing pavilions, beautiful buildings and statues. Tu Duc's tomb was off to one side, as though you were invited to relax and enjoy yourself on the way to pay your respects. We were told he was an avid fisherman and had spent many of his days there long before he died. It was easy to imagine small groups of the rich and famous relaxing and socializing in the idyllic setting.

Back in Da Nang, we visited Marble Mountain and the beautiful gulf beach nearby. We were scheduled to stay at a new, modern-appearing hotel on the beach but it had been closed for lack of business. The entire staff was in a meeting when we arrived, the subject being how to drum up more business.

We arrived in Hanoi early the next afternoon. No one met us at the airport. By 3:00 P.M., when they closed and locked up the arrival terminal, I decided it was time to initiate some action. We were sitting on the curb with our bags. There were no taxis to Hanoi, possibly because of the distance involved (about 55 kilometers). Besides, I had no idea of where to go in Hanoi since no hotel was specified on our itinerary.

There were several people in the departure area but not one admitted to understanding any English. A very tough appearing, unusually large man approached us and indicated that he would drive us to Hanoi for $20.00. The price wasn't bad but the odds of arriving with any money or personal possessions, or even arriving at all, didn't look too great. I declined, then asked him where I could find a telephone (one hand on an ear, the other making dialing motions). He shook his head and waved his hands indicating there wasn't any.

It was true that I hadn't seen a phone in the departure and arrival areas but I refused to believe that an airport terminal that large would not have a phone to Hanoi. I asked Tracy to stay close to the bags while I began a full-scale search. On the far side of the departure area, there was a small red building about three by six feet square with lots of windows and a full-length counter inside. On the counter was a dial-less phone. It, like the rest of the room, was dusty and dirty. A young lady sat at a counter near the door to the room. I pointed to the phone, held my hand up to one ear and said, "Hanoi?" She nodded yes.

I dug out a paper our agent in Bangkok had given me that had the telephone number of the Vietnam Tourism office in Hanoi. After motioning me into the room, she dialed the number on a phone she had under her counter. Another wave told me I should pick up the phone. I said, "Hello?" Only static greeted my anxious ear. I yelled, "Hello!" More static. I screamed, "HELLO!!" A very faint human sound came back, mixed with the static. I screamed, "Is this the Vietnam Tourism office?" I heard something that sounded more like a "yes" than a "no." To make a long story short, after ten minutes and a sore throat, I thought they knew some tourists were at the airport who wanted a ride to a hotel.

The man on the other end of the line was trying to give me some numbers but it was impossible to distinguish them from the constant background static. I decided they pertained to a bus number and one of the numbers was probably a 'seven.' Not much to go on. The young lady collected some money from me and wrote out a little receipt. We waited an hour. Still no bus. I called again and received the same unintelligible message. About 5:00 P.M., a comparatively new bus pulled in and parked at the other end of the terminal. I walked over and asked if he was there to pick us up. The driver understood enough, shook his head and denied knowing anything about us. His last word was, "Norwegians."

Tracy and I discussed the possibilities. The bus license number had a 'seven' in it and he was probably there to pick up some Norwegians. That was enough. We dragged our bags over to the bus; he motioned us to the back.

A little later, another airplane landed and soon a group of about fifteen Norwegians climbed into the bus. Their guide, also Norwegian, walked to the back, counting noses, and noticed us. He asked, "English?" I said, "United States." It would be difficult to describe the look on his face (other than a frown) but the message was clear: "What the hell are you doing here?"

The ride into town was slow and rough. About 8:00 P.M., we stopped in front of a hotel. The man who was to be our guide in

Hanoi, Mr. Thun, met us and explained that the hotel was full and some other arrangements would have to be made. I asked if we could find something to eat while that was being done; we didn't get a lunch on the airplane and were hungry.

He sat at another table in the dining room with a group of young Vietnamese men involved in a loud discussion which, we thought, contained a lot of jokes about us because of the many glances at us after some punch lines and laughs. We finished our omelets and waited while their discussion continued. After about thirty minutes, I decided it was time to take the initiative. I went over and asked him to please come to our table and have a seat, there were some things that had to be discussed. He shrugged and said he'd be there in a few minutes. The discussion continued and my blood pressure went up. Tracy wasn't feeling well and my patience was wearing a little thin.

I started over to his table a second time. He saw me coming but continued talking with his friends as though my presence was of absolutely no concern to him. Bending down close to his ear, I told him is as level a voice as I could manage that my son was ill, that we had been patient enough and I wanted immediate action regarding some accommodations. He nodded and said he would be only a few minutes. About five minutes later, he sauntered over to our table, a very hostile person, stood in front of us with his hands on his hips and said:

"Well, Mr. Brown, you bomb our people, destroy our land and now you want service?" (How did he know I was in the Air Force in Vietnam?)

"Mr. Thun, my son and I have traveled half way around the world out of concern for your country and your people. I do not believe your behavior is appropriate."

"If your concern for us is so great, why did you come over here and bomb us?"

"I was a member of the military forces and had to obey the orders of my government just like the men in your army that invaded South Vietnam."

It was a 30-minute nose-to-nose confrontation. The thing that made the largest impression was that we had paid for the trip ourselves. He had a hard time understanding how any travel abroad was possible without government sponsorship.

The argument was stimulating and I felt some progress was being made in getting him to understand our motivations for the trip but it wasn't moving us any closer to a room. I stood up and said we were moving from the restaurant to the lobby. They had big, overstuffed chairs there and we would simply spend the night in them. He could be sure that next morning I would be in touch with the Vietnam Tourism office and they would be aware of my complete dissatisfaction with our treatment in Hanoi.

That last message got his attention. He apologized for letting his personal feelings affect his job and headed for a telephone. A few minutes later he returned and announced that we would stay at another hotel. I wanted to know if it was a hotel for tourists. He said no, but he was sure we would be satisfied. I wondered. After our encounter, being somewhat at his mercy for, at least, the night, he could put us in some ratty (literally) quarters for revenge. It was about 11:00 P.M. and we were tired so I agreed.

This time our car was one of those big, black Russian sedans. Everything on it flopped and rattled but it ran. We seemed to be wandering around the dark streets. I couldn't keep track of directions after a while, so it was time to sit back and enjoy the sights, which consisted primarily of bicycle riders passing through dim headlight beams. At one point, there was a high wall running along one side of the street. Mr. Thun turned around and looked at me with a gleam in his eyes, pointed to the wall and said, "Hanoi Hilton."

We crossed an open area then passed through a small village and turned left, going down a narrow lane with trees and bushes brushing the car on both sides. A massive solid steel gate in a high wall loomed up in the headlights and we stopped. One door swung open slightly and a guard emerged. He walked up to the car and there was some conversation. The guard was satisfied, he stepped back and yelled something. A series of long groans came from their hinges as both doors swung open. In the back of the car, Tracy and I were doing a little mental groaning too. Did we want to go in there? Would we ever get out again, or would we become just two more missing Americans? The decision to visit Vietnam had been made months ago, the only thing we could do was live with our decision. Panic at that time would not do us any good and would probably give our guide some satisfaction I didn't want him to have.

To put it mildly, we were interested in where we were going so both of us watched intently as the car moved forward. The bumpy blacktop road turned into a curving, smooth brick lane with concrete curbs and cut grass beyond them. Soon we came to a parking area in front of a long, modern three-story building with many large windows. Only a few lights were on inside and no people were around. We turned down another lane and traveled in lazy curves between beautiful, large, two-story residences with dimly lit porches and drive-through porticoes.

I asked Mr. Thun for some information about the place. Even in the dark it looked like something very special. He said it was the living quarters for politburo members when it was in session. Right now, it was adjourned and he had received permission for us to stay there while we were in Hanoi.

We pulled up in front of one of the residences. Even at that late hour, we were met by a housekeeper and several servants. They escorted us upstairs. Small women, weighing about ninety pounds, tried to drag the bags up while our driver and guide just watched. Tracy and I went back and got them. Only two bedrooms occupied the entire floor. My bathroom was larger then our bedroom at home. The bedroom, with its polished wood floor, looked more like a roller skating rink with a bed in the middle. Furnishings were luxurious. Through the windows and trees I could see lights reflecting on water. We were near a lake. I took a good hot bath in the huge tub and went to bed. Sleep did not come quickly – I kept thinking about how we had fallen down in a pile of brown stuff and come out smelling like a rose.

Next morning our guide was cooperative, friendly and, for the most part, less suspicious of our goals. I asked him many questions about his life. He, like our Saigon guide, was formerly an English teacher. Somehow, he managed to retain a student status during the war and was never a member of the army. I suspected that his parents were influential communists. He had been a teacher for several years but, after marriage and a baby, found it was impossible to eke out reasonable existence on his salary and all the odd jobs he could find. Thun didn't say exactly how he managed to get the guide job but I decided it took his parents, a bribe or a combination of both.

When we started talking about careers in Vietnam, he became even more emotional than during our nose-to-nose the night before. His frustrations were obvious. Sometimes his face was contorted and it was hard to understand him as he spoke through clenched teeth. Once he hit the dashboard with his fist. I felt sorry for him. A key point in the many inequities covered was wages. He had earned a degree in a difficult subject and completed many extra courses to qualify as an English teacher yet his pay was only 6,000 dong per month – about $2.00 U.S. At that pay level, regardless of the universal rice allowance for all Vietnamese, free medical care, and low-rent housing, it was impossible to provide his family with proper food and clothing. Purchasing one of the poorly made Vietnamese bicycles was a major investment, comparable to buying a new car in the States.

Our first stop that morning was Ho Chi Minh's tomb. Fortunately, it was closed. I had heard that tourists had been man-handled and even detained for not affording Ho proper respect, such as passing his casket with head not bowed or hands not at sides. The huge polished marble building was dwarfed by two towering construction cranes behind it. I asked Thun what was being built. It was going to be a museum and memorial for Ho Chi Minh. He added that it was the largest current construction project in Vietnam. Give the peasants hype, not opportunity.

Next we walked over to Ho's little cottage-like home in a nearby grove of trees where he had preferred to live during his later years. It was a simple wood-framed residence, configured the same as dwellings I'd seen in Laotian villages. The frame consisted of wood posts set in the ground with an upper floor that contained a small library, a bedroom, bath and rudimentary kitchen. Large screened windows let the breezes flow through while shutters afforded some privacy in his bedroom. The concrete covered lower floor was completely open on three sides, just a low step up from the ground. Its only furniture was a large but unpretentious conference table and straight chairs. I imagined what it would have been like – small groups of people following winding paths through the trees to meet at a long, shaded table, sunlight filtering down and birds singing, Uncle Ho descending the steps to meet them and teach, something he was very good at. I could see how the austere furnishings, retreat-like atmosphere, natural environment (a very unnatural place for business and political conferences) could get visitors' attention, make a deep impression and imbue more objectiveness to the discussions. Ho Chi Minh was a patriot and one smart fellow.

I couldn't help comparing his home with the luxurious accommodations current politburo members had made for themselves. Also, Ho's home had no walls around it; the politburo's residences had water on three sides and a high wall on the fourth, with guards pacing back and forth on the full perimeter day and night. I doubted Uncle Ho would be pleased with the way some things had gone since his death.

Our next stop was named 'Revolutionary Museum' but its format and theme was very similar to the war museum we'd seen in Saigon. We were escorted into one room devoted entirely to war atrocities. I didn't see any photos of the three thousand people executed in Hue. Tracy called my attention to the fact that the faces of all troops photographed in the act of committing represented atrocities had been crudely touched up to show Caucasian features, regardless of their uniforms. Once again, we were told how the North Vietnamese had driven out the American invaders in 1975.

Tracy and I listened, saying nothing until we were out in the hall. It was time for Mr. Thun and I to have another nose-to-nose conversation. This one was much calmer, more objective. It went something like this:

"Mr. Thun, you have two eyes and I have two eyes. Most likely, we would never see an event exactly the same way. We have listened to your explanation of the war. Would you be at all interested in how I saw it?"

His answer was a surprisingly positive "Yes."

I explained that, from my view, the United Nations recognized the South Vietnamese government had been threatened by another nation; that the United States and other nations had volunteered assistance; that the war had become increasingly unpopular with our people; that, with a democratic form of government, United States leaders were forced to withdraw our armed forces, the last combat units leaving in 1973; and that the only forces the NVA met during their 1975 invasion were South Vietnamese. I explained that, in my eyes, they were the invaders.

I went on to mention that nothing Americans did during the war which might be construed as 'atrocities' could begin to match the things Vietnamese did to each other. My concluding statement was that, so far as I could see, neither North nor South Vietnam people were better off for all their sacrifices. No one had really won anything. No one.

Thun's head was nodding frequently in acknowledgment, possibly agreement, of my statements. From that moment until he waved good-bye at the airport, all propaganda efforts stopped and we enjoyed the opportunity to learn more about the Vietnamese people, its rich history and current problems.

A chance encounter at noon that day was very interesting and, ultimately, revealing. Tracy and I were standing in a small park waiting for Mr. Thun while he was picking up some tickets for a circus we were going to see that night. Two attractive, well-dressed, middle-aged ladies, involved in a discussion, were walking towards us on the sidewalk. As they passed in front of us, one said in perfect English, "Good morning. Isn't it a beautiful day?" I replied, "Yes, the weather is perfect and the park is beautiful." She stopped instantly, turned around and said, "You *do* speak English. Where are you from?" My reply was, "The United States."

You could see she wasn't prepared for my answer. Her head jerked a little and she let out a sound of surprise. After a few moments she asked us why we were there. My answer was that we were just tourists, interested in the Vietnamese people and how they were faring after years of war. She obviously wanted to talk more so, after introductions, we strolled a little way into the park. To preserve the privacy of the two women, I will not describe them except to say that the one who spoke fluent English had been educated in France and currently lived outside of Vietnam. She was involved in an aid program for the Vietnamese.

She wanted to know our backgrounds; Tracy's doctorate in psychology impressed her. My presidency of an engineering firm fully involved in manufacturing sciences didn't mean much. I suggested interest in supporting development of a technical manufacturing base in Vietnam and mentioned I would consider a role in any effort to achieve that end.

At one point, I suggested that a "Marshall Plan" type program should be established for Vietnam to get it in a sound economic condition. She bristled at this idea and said such a program could only be considered if there was absolutely no interference with Vietnam's internal affairs. My reply was that Japan and West Germany certainly weren't hurting as a result of their Marshall Plan assistance.

I noticed that her friend stood a distance away from us and both had a habit of looking around, even while talking. After about fifteen minutes, she explained that a long talk with us in a public place could put her friend in an awkward position and may affect her own relationship with the government. After a hasty exchange of addresses, they left.

A few months later, I was surprised to receive a phone call from her. She was in the States on a mission for her Vietnamese aid program and wanted Tracy's current phone number. Later Tracy told me she wanted him to return to Vietnam to fill some not very well defined function. Dropping out of his current research and academic projects would be too costly, so he had to decline the offer. The experienced industrialist in technical fields wasn't invited. It looked as though nothing had changed since 1968 – the peasants couldn't and the wealthy wouldn't. Like China, the distribution of power and wealth after the war remained the same, only the names and titles were different.

The balance of our time in Hanoi was spent in roaming the area with a few visits to ancient historical sites. We asked to stop at a book store in downtown Hanoi and found several books in English. Prices were in dongs and, to my surprise, dollars. One, entitled *Vietnam*, written and published in Moscow, looked interesting. I purchased it so I could learn the communist version of Vietnamese history. Near the center of the book were two large photographs on facing pages. One showed a group of smiling, relaxed NVA troops standing in front of a monument. The description with the photo said, "The People's Army of Vietnam completed their victorious offensive, which culminated in the liberation of the south of the country. The last inch of land of Vietnam had been cleared of foreign occupiers."

The other pictured American prisoners of war in a line, getting into an airplane for their trip back home. The caption read, "Yet another group of Americans are leaving Vietnam forever. In conformity with the agreement between Vietnam and the USA, these would-be conquerors were given a chance to return home. They have been lucky. During the years of the 'dirty war' against the people of Vietnam, thousands of American soldiers went back home in regulation army coffins."

South Vietnam became a separate nation back in 1620, when the ruler of a province near Hue stopped paying taxes to Hanoi. Between 1627 and 1673, several large invasions were attempted by the north but all were repelled. Two high walls, one eleven miles and one six miles long, were instrumental in the successful defense of the south. Incidentally, they were in the same area as the DMZ. Finally, both sides signed a truce in 1673, designating the Linh River as the border. 'Liberation of the south from the foreign invader', really?

During our travels around Hanoi, we saw two disturbances; major conflicts between people that involved screaming, pushing and raw emotional displays. Both were being closely observed by groups of people who appeared to be participating to some extent in the 'discussions.' The first one we saw was in the outskirts of town, near where we parked to buy something. It was between two women. Mr. Thun shrugged off our questions as though it simply wasn't important enough to be concerned about and we left without learning anything about the issue.

The second altercation was a little different. It was on a corner in the downtown shopping area and the issue was between a young policeman and a middle-aged man standing next to a moped. People standing in a circle around them were yelling too, waving their arms and jostling each other as they vied for front line positions. I asked Mr. Thun to please tell me something about the issue involved. He hesitated then began an explanation. The first part we had heard several times before, that the Vietnam civil police were corrupt, stopping anyone they chose and demanding money, cigarettes or whatever they desired, with the only alternative being jail. They have authority to arrest and fine people at the point of infraction without the right to trial or review by a judge. In this particular case, the policeman claimed the driver had made an illegal turn on his moped and was demanding an amount of money considered exorbitant by him and many in the crowd. It's tough to win an argument when your opponent holds all the aces and the gun. I hoped that individual, with the courage to stand up to a corrupt policeman, didn't end up in jail.

Two other incidents that occurred in Hanoi were interesting. While driving slowly through a crowded market area, a boy, about ten years old, stepped out of the crowd and spit on our windshield. Later, traveling in the countryside, a young man threw a stone at the car. Tracy didn't appreciate their actions but I reminded him that we were two

Caucasians traveling in a Russian car and the insults were aimed at Russia, not us. I couldn't blame them. If I had to live at the level they were, I'd probably do the same thing.

One tends to regard peasants as herds of people, not individuals capable of creative thought, with goals and abilities that could extend far beyond their typical life patterns. Only education and opportunity separate them from the middle class and wealthy. The phrase, "There but for the grace of God, go I" is almost right. Only "There but for the circumstances at birth, go I" separates me from the rock-throwing peasant. I felt for him.

Beginning with our first few hours in Saigon and continuing right up to the airport gate at Hanoi, we were impressed with the large number of permanent war memorials that had been constructed or still in the works. In a country so desperately in need of an industrial base, why spend so much money on memorials? Why was the largest construction project of all a museum? Tracy and I concluded that the government was trying to maintain a spirit of post-war/recovery so that people would be more likely to accept the lower standards afforded them.

Back in Bangkok, we met a Thai merchant who had done business in Vietnam for several years. His comments were interesting. First, he said Vietnam government officials were totally corrupt, that absolutely nothing happened without a substantial bribe. The primary activities of government offices and officials were maneuvers designed to place them in positions where more bribes would have to come their way. With enough money under the counter, one could do almost anything in Vietnam so long as it didn't threaten officials' authority or income.

Names change, titles change but relationships remain the same in Vietnam and most of the Far East nations. Poor are born for exploitation; rich are born to exploit. Neither Vietnam nor the rest of the world will remember for long the sacrifices Americans made to improve (at least ostensibly) opportunities for the people of that nation because we didn't accomplish a single thing. Other than getting 58,000 Americans killed and providing memories for survivors, it was a tragic waste fostered by incompetent leaders, political and military.

APPENDICES

Appendix A

Hue Battle Tapes

[Thirty minutes of heavy fighting, rockets, mortars, machine guns, etc., then my voice.]

It's precisely noon on the thirty-first of January, and the other side [of the tape] is the some of the sound effects of the attack on our compound, beginning about five minutes after the attack started. Maybe even ten minutes. I haven't listened to it and I don't know whether the rocket rounds were still coming in then or not. There's still plenty of fight going around but we're not taking any incoming here in the compound so I'm back up in my room. Thought I'd get a few words on tape then I'm going to get some sleep. The room's a mess. I wondered whether I should even send this tape to you or even make the tape. I may not send it to you. I haven't made up my mind yet. At least you would worry, but I know you're going to worry anyway. [Airplane sounds] Stand by one.

One O-2 came down below the clouds momentarily and I'm hoping he can get over to House Eight. I think it's probably Jenkins and I want him to see if anything can be found over at House Eight. We had radio contact with House Eight until five o'clock in the morning, then we lost contact. I'm real worried about them because they don't have too good a defense over there.

I'm just taking off my left boot – I had glass in both my boots when I pulled them on. Oh, gee, had a pile of glass in that one. Funny I didn't have any – my God – funny I didn't get more cuts; I thought my foot would be bloody but it's not. The other one was so bad with glass I had to stop and take it off before I could even walk.

We got hit with 140mm rockets [later reported to be 122mm] and the usual mortars. The first 140mm rocket hit right on the TOC [Tactical Operations Center], right across the street from us here, on the top of the roof. That's the one that woke me up and I rolled off along the side the bed. Nothing came in for a few seconds so I said, "Well, I'd better get up and get some clothes on; guess we're going to be around for a while." I got up and I was standing in the middle of the room – I don't know what I was doing now but I was walking – anyway, I was standing in the middle of the room and one hit right outside, in the barbed wire by the gate and blew up several jeeps. And hit the room with such force that it even blew barbed wire clear inside the room here. Through closed windows and screens, no less. Lots of shrapnel in the room and I was, honestly speaking, very lucky to get missed. Well, I got hit by glass. I got, I guess, ten cuts on me from flying glass but none of them serious, all of them scratches except one on the palm of my hand where I hit the floor. That one bled but not bad at all. Then I got my flying suit on, my boots on and started to go to the command post and I thought, "My God, I think I'll just tape this thing," so I came back in here and turned the tape recorder on and then left. Well, I stayed on the balcony for, I guess, twenty minutes or so until I finally screwed up enough courage to take that hundred yard dash, well, hundred-foot dash, across the open place, down the open staircase, and across the open part of the compound to get to the command bunker.

Right now, NVA occupy some buildings and school buildings around here on several sides. In fact, the school building right next door to the compound here on the southeast side – they were in there, shooting at us, and I guess they were going to use that as a primary position but we put so many rounds in that building, it's really ventilated. B-70s, M-79s, and oh, well, the building is still standing but it's definitely ventilated much better than it was before this attack started.

Well, we just got the word by radio – [Wham!]

Oops! Damn. We just got the word by radio that Jenson took a low pass over the airport and he took a lot of fire and that all of the airplanes on the field are either damaged or destroyed so we're going to put some gunships in on the field and just really total the place. [Whiz. Bam.]

Well, I do think I'll bend over a little bit lower anyway and put my flak jacket back on. What the hell was that? I've moved the tape recorder around to the other side of the room because it's definitely getting hot on that side.

We have been beset by heavy fog that rolled in after the attack began. It was like beautiful timing on the part of the NVA. By about fifteen minutes after dawn, it was like pea-soup fog all over the place. It stayed down until about ten o'clock; we got our first medivac out about eleven. And another one out about twelve. [Boom!] Wow!

It's fifteen hundred, same day [January 31] and shades of the old Indians surrounding the fort and the cavalry arrives to save them all. They blow the bugles and charge down the hill, scattering the Indians to the four winds and save the fort. I hope we live happily ever after. The Marines have landed – the Marine reaction force –after a fierce fire fight and losing one tank – has arrived at the compound now, within the last few minutes, with five tanks and they've put one on each corner and they've got another one out scouting. Oh, those big things look nice! Damn, those tanks look good. It certainly changes the complexion of the battle. There's about fifteen helicopters circling overhead and I think they have first Air Cav troops or Marine troops in them to land as a forward reaction force. Boy, I hope they come in here because we were not looking forward to this evening. Or this night. Also we managed to get in a heli-lift of ammunition and all of the wounded have been medivac-ed. They have the last bunch going out now, the third helicopter load. They just put them on the truck to haul them over to the place where they can land, next to the river that's not getting too much fire. Well, I'll tell you, I just about choked up, when those Marines came down the road with those tanks. God, they looked good!

Well, it's the morning of the first of February now. And we got through the long night successfully. We had quite a few wounded; we evaced, put twelve in a helicopter, in a wild, hairy landing down here in the fog, about one o'clock this morning. I found out why those 105mm shells were sent in – they were for the tanks that are now in town. The night, compared to the night before, was relatively quiet. We had no rocket attacks. Well, we got, I guess, thirty or forty mortars put in on us, but dug in like we are, it does nothing but make noise. I don't think a single person was wounded at all from the mortar attacks, but we did get some wounding from other actions. Just before dark, we sent out an expedition of Marines to go around to House Eight and the other outlying houses here and pick up the troops that were out there, including my Air Force troops, and bring them in here to the compound. And they didn't make it. They got attacked with B-40s, which are rockets, and guns, and they just didn't make it.

We had at least one airplane over us almost all the night, throwing out flares, keeping the place illuminated. Although when the fire was the thickest, it was kind of tough. We didn't get much illumination from the flares. But any was better than none. And I think it may have helped to substantially reduce our losses last night because they really didn't get a chance to creep up on us and hit us as hard as they could have, had they had the advantage of complete darkness.

Got nineteen more wounded to haul out today. First thing this morning. We're running low on medical supplies and we're very low on ammunition. I tell you what, we're in siege really, is what it amounts to, except the helicopter allows us to get some stuff. We have no water, or running low on water, we had a trailer-load –[Bang. Wham.]

Wow. Getting some action . . . Running low on everything, food, water, medical supplies.

The tank couldn't make it between here and House Eight, which is two blocks from here. It was set on fire by the B-40s. You can't say, really, that it's a no sweat situation yet but it's not so bad. I'm not worried about capture and surrender of the whole compound. There was a Spooky around ten o'clock last night (that's the flare ship), said there was a big fire fight going on over at the field. Much firing across the runway and that the white house, which is Lt. Koung's house, on the left side of the field, went up in flames. Then about four o'clock this morning, Division reported that the area around the field was a mass of very high flames. I don't know what's left over there. Probably not much.

The yard down here is full of wounded. They captured ten NVA in civilian clothes over here right at the corner of our compound this morning at dawn. I saw them out there, I saw the ARVN around them. I didn't know what the hell was going on except maybe they were hauling in some civilian refugees, but it turned out that they were NVA that were captured right there. Apparently they got pinned down by us, all the light we had last night, and couldn't get out because they'd come underneath our fire. When light [day] came and they realized they were dead pigeons, they just stood up and gave up. This is a newly infiltrated NVA unit that has come in here and it's got nothing but the very best equipment. They came in here to do a job, you can see that.

Standing out here on the balcony is like having a grandstand seat on the war. Everything is flying and tearing around. There's a helicopter picking up more wounded over there by the river and then there are two gunships circling around here at tree-top height to protect the helicopter on the ground making the pick-up. Two helicopters gunships with rockets and fifty cals on them. We have one FAC up in the air, an O-2, Lopez [call-sign], from down south of Da Nang. He made a pass at about fifteen hundred feet, over the citadel part of the city and boy, he caught ground fire – man, the whole place opened up on him. I expected to see him come down in flames, but he didn't. We got a damage report from [the] Lopez [FAC], flying low over the field, over where he could see, anyway, and three O-2s are totally destroyed, one of them is still standing, but I doubt if it is flyable. One O-1 is destroyed, totally, and three of them are still standing. The POL system, our fuel supply system, is totally destroyed. About half of the Army O-1s are destroyed and all of the VNAF choppers are destroyed.

[Sustained firing in background for several minutes. No voice.]

In broad daylight, yet. We just got a little attack from the buildings around the side of the compound here. It's getting to be quite a fire fight. A helicopter flew over and they opened up on it first; I think that's what got the whole thing started.

I said I was going to lay down and take a nap this afternoon. I did lay down, several times, for up to as long as five minutes at a time. It's just impossible to get a nap here. They're clearing out the buildings immediately around the compound. The schoolhouse on the back side of the compound is burning, the buildings along the side have been riddled. They've been using a tank, with the 105mm gun on the front of it, right by the side of the building here, going WHAM! They've [the VNAF] been bombing, now, in the downtown area across the river, and every time one of those bombs hits, the whole building bounces about six inches and, to put it mildly, conditions are not conducive to sleeping.

According to the latest figures I can find, by noon today, there were supposed to have been five battalions, which is a regiment, of NVA inside the walled city. And there are two battalions of 101st ARVN Airborne inside the walls and two more trying to get in. It's going to be a real bash. They said they'd counted four hundred to five hundred bodies already this morning, by lunch. They're taking their casualties too. I know there's a lot of ARVN wounded too. But on this side of the river, there's a lot of Marines wounded and killed. I've seen five or six bodies so far. And some very seriously injured. They just brought in two more truckloads of injured that just left the compound two hours ago to start this little sweep. They still haven't gotten the people out of House Eight, the Air Force people. They got to within about a block of it. They had two tanks, about seventy-five to a hundred Marines and they could not go an inch farther. It was just too hot. So those boys are still out there and they're running low on ammo and running low on water and food and things are getting kind of tight. Tomorrow we've got to get them out of there. I just don't know yet how we're going to do it. They'll sure have something to tell their kids, if they do get out of there all right. It's been quite a fight.

[Crack, crack] A helicopter just flew over and you could hear the NVA shooting at him. [Lots of AK-47 fire.]

Friday morning, February 2, 1968

The first sound you hear will be the mortar going off; the second the mortar impacting. Now they just stopped firing the mortars. They're mortaring a place here on the southeast corner of the compound. It's been causing some trouble during the night. It's Friday morning and they've been mortaring for about ten minutes. I finally decided to put a tape on and they quit. It seems the NVA got back up pretty close to the compound during the night and we've got to do the same process as yesterday, weeding out the immediate perimeter.

[Sounds of weapons firing]

An AK-47 real close to here is shooting now and I wanted to catch that – There, that's an AK-47 there. It's a very characteristic sound and I wanted you to hear it. You'll recognize it. Wow! That big bang must have been a tank. I hope.

Okay. The mortars are going again. Now you can hear that real well, I think. They're mortaring from right beside the barracks here and hitting a place about one hundred yards from here. Jeez, not everyone could sit up in their room, drink hot chocolate and watch a war going on like this.

I was going to spend some time to make you a nice tape this morning but things haven't calmed down very much. I think this is going to be a very lively day. We lost an awful lot of Marines yesterday. Really tragic, this house to house fighting is terrifying and extremely bad for people moving on the street because the enemy can sit in the house in a relatively invulnerable position, in complete secrecy, and just snipe away and pick off the soldiers at their leisure. It's strictly murder. I don't know how many are dead but we've been hauling a lot of bodies and there are bodies laying out here by the tennis court now. It's just real rough. There's just no way to get out of it. We have more reinforcements coming in today so I've no doubt but what we'll win but I can't say that was always my feeling. I felt fairly secure all the time but I was damned glad to see the reinforcements arrive. The night was relatively quiet. No mortar attacks on us.

Do you hear those AK-47s? They're shooting from that school building they burned down yesterday afternoon. Didn't do much good to burn it down. The top floor didn't fall out. Now you're hearing a real drama there; someone fighting for his life. We've got overwhelming fire-power over these guys with their small guns but they got into town and are well secreted and it's going to take a lot to get them out. In this kind of a war, it's an eye for an eye and a tooth for a tooth. If you don't want to give up a hundred dead for getting a hundred dead the only other way to do it is sheer fire-power. It's expensive but it saves lives. And that's what I'm for right now, saving lives. I see all these kids being hauled out under the covers and you just are reminded of the price so many must pay. It gets down right sad sometimes.

They're firing from both sides now. [loud battle sounds] do believe I'll get down a little bit lower. In fact, it seems some glass came into my room here. I don't know but what they're trying to level the joint. You can't say it's a dull breakfast. Not one bit. They're sure peppering the school but hell, that guy is down behind the concrete and they're not going to get him that easy. They're going to have to get the one-oh-fives in here and blow down a few walls. Or get a good shot with a grenade.

Well, things are a little quieter now. I qualified for a Purple Heart. This morning I went over to the medic's before the line of dead and wounded coming in was too great and they looked at my hand. Had to sew up my palm.

Oh, damn it. There goes another racket. Somebody's still shooting at us. I got hit by all that glass, you know. Most of it isn't very bad but there's a cut on one hand they had to put a few stitches in so what do you know? Purple Heart. I didn't plan to get one but if that's all it's going to be, I'm happy. Believe me!

The morning the whole attack started, which was the 31st, midst all the smoke and confusion of that first attack, which was a wild one, here came a great big white goose walking up the road towards our compound. The doors of the compound were open, they were getting someone in, I forget who, and – [big bang]

Wow! That was a B-40. I'll put my hat back on. I'd taken it off. I think I'll move into the other room; it's a little safer in there.

Anyway this big white goose came walking up the street and walked right into the compound. I don't know where he came from;

I've never seen him around here before. He's not from this area. He has been in the compound ever since, just honking his way around. I tried to make friends with him one time and he chased me half-way across the compound. Nobody fools with him; he's a mean son of a gun. We throw him crackers and crumbs and I guess he's getting enough to eat. He's just made himself at home. Last night he spent the night outside the CP and if you go outside in the middle of the night, he'll just be sitting there. Just made himself comfy.

The Marines are lined up now and are moving out. We got the tanks going and I don't know what percent of those Marines are going to come back tonight. Last night when they came in, they were dragging a bunch of their bodies. They had no stretchers. And dragging some of the wounded. It's just real rough. That's all you can say for it. They're trying to get out the front door of the compound right now and having a lot of trouble doing that. The NVA has moved in now, apparently to bottle us in. We'll get out; it may cost us a few but we'll make it.

House Eight is still okay. I don't know how they managed to survive as long as they have but they're out of water completely, out of food completely and very low on ammunition. Sometime today we're going to try to arrange a drop of food and water, and ammunition, into the compound. And some M-79 grenade launchers. I don't know if we're going to be able to get them in there or not because the NVA are so solid around there that I don't think a chopper can get down that low to the ground and ever get back up. I really don't think so.

This will be an experience. I wouldn't care to do it again but I wouldn't miss it. It's exciting to put it mildly. I have trouble sleep during the day, just because I have to get up and see what's going on. The windows are all shot out up here on the northwest end of the hotel. [big bang]

Oh! That's the one-oh-five going off there. People are shooting out all the windows, the furniture is all torn up, the walls are all pock-marked with bullets. Honest to God, it's better than any movie I've ever seen.

The Marines didn't make it out of the compound. They're retreating back inside the gate. It's pretty rough when you can't even get out your front door. They really moved in in force last night. I don't know what we're going to do now; we'll figure out something. May have to call in airstrikes and level the joint.

Friday afternoon, February 2, 1968

[First two sentences were Janice's, not erased before starting my tape.]

[Janice:] Lands sakes alive. What am I going to talk about for fifteen minutes tonight?

[Dick:] Well, you may have that problem but I don't. It's 4:00 in the afternoon on the second of February and it's been an absolutely frantic day again. Words could never describe. I have no film but I could have taken a million pictures that would be interesting. And I don't have a single one. It's been another day of enlightenment, some sadness and, well, excitement. We had about three or four hours when we could have put in fighters but because of an entanglement and the problem of coordination of the air strikes between the Marines, the ARVN and Army, we only put in one strike late in the afternoon – finished up just a few minutes ago when the weather socked in – then we had to break it off. We have it on the highest information tonight that there will be a max effort against the MACV compound and the Thua Thien Sector Headquarters. So, it ought to be an exciting evening.

The goose is still alive and wandering around but he spent the afternoon sitting by the mortar tubes and I don't think he can hear very well now. He didn't have any fingers to stick in his ears. He's settling down, really; he was nibbling on some grass this afternoon. They're mortaring, you know, wham, bam, wham, bam, and the cannons were firing around there, the tanks, that is, fifty caliber guns yakking away and he's there, tugging on the grass, trying to eat it. And there's not much grass in the whole compound. I think he's getting kinda' hungry.

We didn't lose quite so many troops today. A little more reason prevailed in the effort to recover ground. They shot a lot more and lost a lot less lives, which I was sure glad to see. We didn't gain much territory today, only a few houses in the immediate vicinity and they killed NVA within, oh Lord, from my radio jeep, I guess it was fifty or seventy-five feet to where the NVA were killed and the area around there. They were right up against the fence this morning. We had no idea what a precarious position was like until we tried to go out the gate and found out we were getting sniped at from all sides and very close.

Got some more reinforcements today; came in about half an hour ago. Have those big quad-fifty millimeter guns which are horrendous – [sound of airplane]

Oops. Here comes an O-2 over low. Wish that guy'd get out of here. He's going to get himself shot full of holes in nothing flat.

You know, it looks to me, after watching this war going on, these Marines' best situation is to get wounded. The ideal situation is to get wounded and not killed. That way you get out of the fighting, at least for a while, without getting killed. If they can just manage to avoid the fatal punch, they'd be in good shape. But that's pretty hard to do.

I'm getting used to seeing the dead now. At first it was real hard but you can get used to anything after a while.

For the first time today, right now, there's been any degree of quiet in the immediate area of the compound. We've just been shooting up a storm. The compound is practically a solid mass of spent shells. You can walk on brass around here.

[Airplane sounds again.]

Oh, he's getting shot at again. Listen to those shots. They're shooting at my O-2. That's most distressing. They're shooting right across the street. After all the work we've been doing. Not much progress. No sweat. We'll make it.

They've killed many – [airplane sounds again] Oh, God damn it. I've got to go down there [to the radio jeep] and tell that O-2 to get out of here. He's just taking too much ground fire. I think he's leaving now. No, he's not. Stand by one.

I can't find out who that FAC is. He's still buzzing around out there and hasn't been shot down yet but I don't know why. There's quite a fire fight going on again right here at the same street corner in front of our gate. NVA are still in there solid. [Bam] That was a one-oh-five cannon going off then. And we've got these quad-fifties; [combat sounds] that's a fifty caliber machine gun followed by a 105 tank gun. A little ordnance around here. Really, though, this microphone and this tape recorder just doesn't do it justice. Every time that cannon goes off, glass falls out of the windows, the house shakes, it just doesn't do it justice. But, of course, what do you expect with this kind of equipment? Plaster is falling down from the ceiling; I'm just sitting here with the house vibrating every time that thing fires. And this is a concrete building so you get an idea of what kind of concussion it is.

Saturday morning, February 3, 1968

[Poor sentence structure and rambling thoughts were probably the effect of fatigue.]

I have Armed Forces Radio station turned on. Swept my room out. It's Saturday morning, the third of February.

Oh, we had excellent work with the flares last night. I stayed up a good part of the night, working with the flare ships, adjusting them this way and that way, and the last ship we had, starting at one o'clock in the morning, he was a jewel. He laid those flares down exactly where we wanted them and he was flying instruments above the clouds, the flares were dropping down through the clouds – which were down only about three or four hundred feet above the ground. And those flares would zip down one side of the compound and down the other side then down the middle, just back and forth like this. We got him to come over the compound, adjusted them so precisely that they came over the compound at about fifty feet. If there was a blade of grass disturbed or anything there, on any side of the compound, we zapped it when these flares went over it. So there was a lot of shooting during the night.

Pardon me for yawning. I had every right to. My eyes feel like two Ford stoplights. I really haven't jelled any plans on how we're going to operate out of here. We'll figure something out, or we may just give up and operate out of Da Nang. If so, I imagine I'll still stay here and advise, ALO to Gen. Truong. I should because we're going to need an ALO. I've got one pilot left up here –[WHAM!!!]

Jesus Christ! Pardon me, but my God! What a shock. Hold on for a minute.

Well, about ten or fifteen minutes later. They were just blowing up some trees and buildings to get a better field of fire beyond the gate. The Marines are running out of the compound now, in single file, getting down behind the trees, and working their way up the street to start their campaign to weed the VC out of the south side of river of Hue. It's going to be a rough damn operation. I know they're going to haul a bunch of them back on a stretcher today.

Well, our goose is still with us. He doesn't look so good I think he's kind of dry, I think he's kind of hungry, and, last night, why, one time – he doesn't like to be in the dark and he'll come right over to a human and stand beside him if it turns dark. The flares would go out and it would be pitch black in the compound and he'd come trotting over and stand next to me. Flares would come up and he didn't care, he could be anywhere at that time but, boy, he just didn't want to be alone when it was that dark. And he'd sit, oh, ten feet from an 81mm mortar tube, which makes an awfully big bang, but he didn't seem to mind the mortar going off.

Summing the whole thing up, it looks to me like the one thing that's got to be done: they've got to retake A Shau. Because that's where all where all the stuff's getting hauled in from. It comes down by truck through A Shau Valley into the back side of Da Nang. In fact, they have to take the Ho Chi Minh Road, period, if they have to invade Laos to do it. That's how the stuff gets down here, by trucks. Vroom, down the road. Real simple. But the solution isn't simple.

House Eight is on the radio; they're still all alive and healthy. I don't know how they've done it. They reported a few minutes ago that some troops in green fatigues with red arm bands, which are the NVA uniform, passed their house heading towards the river, so maybe the VC are moving out. I hope, I hope, I hope.

What they have been doing is adjusting mortars for the people from here. In other words, where they are, right over in the deep VC target area, they've got one good radio left and so they [the Marines] shoot the mortars and they [the Air Force men] tell them how to correct to hit the houses where the VC are. Which is kind of sneaky, but I like those kind of sneaky people. Yes, sir.

Same day, 1:15 p.m., and the Marines have landed again. More Marines are coming in with all kinds of guns and stuff.

Oh, for God's sake. There goes my last whole window. They blew up a big building here next door that a bunch of sappers were hiding in. We got eighteen sappers, dead in a ditch, within, well, they got them with grenades – they threw grenades at them, within thirty or forty feet of the corner of the compound. They had satchel charges and everything else on them. They came out of a building that's a little farther up the road and they had so many satchel charges in there, stuff and dynamite and all kinds of booby traps and everything like that they'd rigged to go into the compound with, that they decided to simply blow the building up. So they put a charge in there to blow up the building but they forgot about the charge of the TNT. I was downstairs, the adjutant caught me and I was filling out the paperwork for the Purple Heart and, ye gods, all of a sudden, this whole damned building jumped about ten feet and landed and rocks flew down from all over all over the place – big rocks. Just showered the whole compound. They'd forgotten about all the satchel charges and they all went up with the explosion and it was like a small Hiroshima.

It's still Saturday, the third of February – but I just thought I'd tell you. I went down to check with the radio jeep and see what was going on down there and what the situation was with the FACs. I talked to you about that explosion on the last tape and, holy mackerel, it was bigger than I thought it was. The roofs of the buildings down there are ventilated like daylight; the debris, pieces of bricks and stuff like this, are just all over the whole compound. It was a big explosion. And the radio was knocked over and there was nobody around the jeep. I thought sure my radio operator had been hurt so I went tracking him down, through the dispensary and so on, and couldn't find him, never did find him. But the radio was running and everything else so I went ahead with the radio calls I had to make, myself. Holy mackerel, he was lucky, but it ruined that poor old jeep – it was about twenty or thirty feet from one of the [first] rockets and the windshield was smashed, everything is punched full of holes, all but one tire is flat, and it's pretty well beat up. Miraculously, three of the radios still work, HF, UHF and VHF; only the FM was destroyed. Everything was just right, the shrapnel missed that part of the jeep but now, added indignities, it gets poured on by rocks, the roof's cut to pieces; of course, it was already before, but now it's even worse. More dents all over the hood and everything else. That jeep is a wreck! But it still works. Nothing's dull around here, I will say that.

Last night, we wondered why we didn't get an attack on the compound, like they said we were going to. The Marines had set up some mortars in the compound and they'd set up two of them to shoot just a few feet outside the fence. By a few feet, I mean a hundred feet or something like that, outside the fence, on the east side of the compound.

Oh, boy, they found somebody. I was just watching these guys go through these houses. Zap, bam. They throw out a grenade, they run through the windows, they cut inside, and they . . . spray them down with the bullets, and man, that's exciting.

Last night, Capt. Forsyth, who I work with a lot, had the guard post out there in that side and he saw some people moving around in that field. He quick ran over and had them throw out some mortars in that area. They already had them set up, sighted for that thing, and today, they went out there and there are eighteen dead VC. And there were eighteen other dead ones in the gutter where they made the assault the first night. So that's a total of thirty-six of them killed, right outside the fence, on one side of the perimeter. And we're wondering why they aren't they hitting us; well, hell, we killed a bunch of them, at least enough to drive off the attack.

When playing some of this back, some of my speech isn't too clear but I'm very tired and I tend to slur my words.

At any rate, there we were, strolling around inside, discussing things, throwing these mortars out here and there, and we'd gotten eighteen we didn't even know about. Very good.

Sunday, February 4, 1968

Well, would you believe it? Today is Sunday.

Holy mackerel! Things are getting rough. [My radio operator] came running in here and said the radio jeep just got a direct hit with a B-40 round. He was going to call Saigon and he got out of the jeep to start the generator and when he turned around to walk back, the whole jeep just exploded as a B-40 came in (which is a rocket). It wounded four men, including him; some of them are cut up pretty bad but none of them are critical.

Well, I just moved into my other room because some stuff is coming in out there and I don't want to get hit. There's another one. It sounds like they're getting kind of mean. They're hauling the wounded back out from the big battle over here across the street. They're using gas, now, on part of it. We have to stay close to our gas-masks now, which I left in the other room. I'd better get it.

[Bam!!!] Wow! Another B-40 round. We're getting hit. I'm going to duck. A B-40 round just landed right on the dispensary. I don't know how many are hurt over there yet. I'm going to go down on a lower floor; I don't like being on the upper floor right now, so I'll be talking to you again in a little while.

Well, it's much later in the day now; it's a quarter after five. Oh, my God! A quarter after five. The days go by fast! And those nights are so long. Let's see, this is Sunday still and not much has, well, the Marines have made some progress but I don't know what's going to happen tonight, though. Across the river, we have very little knowledge of what's going on over there. And I haven't been able to get across, obviously. We've only had a couple of priority medivacs, and that's the only choppers we've had in today. We just can't seem to get support. The people down at Corps, I think, have no idea what's going on up here. None whatsoever.

Well, that's about the end of this tape; another haphazard tape but, under the conditions, the best I can do.

Appendix B

Excerpts from The Airborne Forward Air Controller Training Manual for the 4410th CCTS

Hurlburt Field, Florida

SECTION B – AIRSTRIKE PROCEDURES

4. One of the most effective applications of airpower in our counterinsurgency effort is the mission performed by the airborne forward air controller (FAC) in his observation aircraft. Our FAC visual reconnaissance program ferrets out the enemy and keeps the enemy off balance, denying him his needed freedom of movement. Also, the selective target control that can be exercised by a forward air controller has greatly enhanced the role of tactical air power in the insurgency situation. This section will present some FAC techniques which have been employed successfully in Vietnam; it is not intended to be either restrictive in nature, nor all-inclusive. No one account can cover all the facets of this diversified mission. However, certain basic techniques have been proved fundamental and will apply to some degree to most tactical situations as modified by the needs of the specific movement. The key to the successful application of tactical air power by an airborne FAC lies in the human equation – the knowledgeable, responsible, trained observation, intelligence, interpretation and action (whether active or passive) by a man. The ability of the man,the FAC, to reason, coupled with his airborne mobility, his knowledge of his tools at hand, fired by individual aggressiveness and self-control have proved over and over to dominate the counterinsurgency battleground. Aggressiveness, discipline, and leadership of the highest degree are demanded from those striving for success in the ever-important role of the FAC.

5. In order to work effectively as a FAC, you must thoroughly understand the capabilities and limitations of the ordnance and the strike aircraft that you direct. You must understand the capabilities and limitations of the troops that you support with particular empha-

sis on the objectives of the ground forces in the current operation. You must be willing to aggressively support their needs, while not over-extending yourself. If you allow yourself to compromise your safety, your troops might find themselves without the value of your immediate services – not to mention that they might have to over-extend themselves in order to aid you. Gallantry, yes, but with discretion. Next, the FAC must completely understand the nature of the enemy, their tactics and their employment of the weapons that he expects to face while controlling his airstrikes. Last, but not least, you must be thoroughly familiar with the terrain you are operating over and with the charts that depict these areas. You are not a trained infantry officer, but you can develop a good comprehension of ground force procedures by forming close associations with the people that you are support and by studying Army publications.

6. For purposes of discussing the FAC mission, the FAC will direct two basic types of airstrikes in the counterinsurgency battle area. The first is direct air support or interdiction; this is not classical interdiction of a strategic nature; rather, these are strikes directed to destroy enemy troops and facilities not in conjunction with a ground force operation. The second type of airstrike is close air support. These are airstrikes in conjunction with a friendly ground operation.

7. One primary mission of the FAC is to support the ground forces by providing them with specialized knowledge of tactical air warfare. In working with the ground forces, you will participate in the following basic operations: attack, defensive, retrograde advance, road clearing and convoy movements, resupply and troop reinforcements, rescue, sweep and clear, and perhaps the most important, search and destroy. Of these, search and destroy operations will be most frequently used in counterinsurgency actions. In each of the above you will provide visual reconnaissance, radio relay, and assistance to the ground forces' precise ground navigation. Most important, however, is that you can provide tactical air strikes tailored to meet the immediate situation, whether it be a pre-strike for a helilift landing zone or close air support.

8. The most important concept that must be grasped by the FAC toward the accomplishment of the mission is that during an airstrike, the FAC is in command of the entire tactical air situation under his immediate control. This is not to detract from the command responsibilities of the fighter flight leader; however,the ultimate command

of the target situation must come from the FAC. The FAC is the pivotal member in a dual command team consisting of himself and the fighter flight leader. The FAC possesses a target within defined limits and with the cooperation of the flight leader, he must employ the fighters to achieve maximum effectiveness. The FAC is responsible to the Air Force, to the ground forces, and to the local populace for the control of the airstrike. The fighters may not strike until they are cleared on target by the FAC and may be called off target by either the flight leader or the FAC should an unreasonable or dangerous situation develop. This "command" implies not only authority but responsibility! Thus is derived fundamental rule #1:

DURING AN AIRSTRIKE THE FAC IS IN COMMAND OF THE TARGET SITUATION.

9. It is axiomatic that the FAC must have compatible communications with his ground forces, the Direct Air Request Net, and with his fighters. You must be thoroughly familiar with all communications facilities and navigation aids available to you. Often, in order to maintain immediate radio contact with the Direct Air Request Net, the FAC will have to operate in a two-ship "formation," one ship flying low with only radio contact with his sister ship who is at a higher altitude and is maintaining contact with the Direct Air Request Net. You must at all times be in radio contact with this command and control facility for a situation might develop requiring you to divert your mission to a higher priority mission. Should you have an emergency develop in flight, the advantages of being in immediate radio contact for self-survival are obvious. In short, fundamental rule #2 is derived: ALWAYS BE IN IMMEDIATE CONTACT WITH THE DIRECT AIR REQUEST NET.

10. The combatants in counterinsurgency usually speak the same language. The capture of a radio will place the insurgent in the position of being able to communicate with aircraft and, in general, raise havoc with orderly communications, ranging from jamming to actually attempting to direct air strikes against friendly positions. The use of authentications and code systems in a hostile environment is mandatory to limit both the interception of friendly instructions by the enemy and to preclude friendly response to fraudulent transmissions. The authentication system may be the published world-wide type or locally established flexible systems. When in doubt, authenticate.

11. In Vietnam the Joint General Staff (JGS) publishes a standard operating instruction directive (SOI) every month or as required. Each FAC will have a copy of the SOI as it contains: (1) Current Army net using frequencies, (2) Encoding and decoding procedures for letters, numerals, common phrases, and often-used locations. This SOI is as much a part of a FAC's tools as the very charts he uses to reconnoiter his area. Be sure to carry a current SOI.

12. Airstrike Tactics:

a. General – The simplified airstrike can be subdivided into five basic parts: (1) Mission preparation, (2) rendezvous, (3) target description and marking, (4) on-target control and (5) the bomb damage assessment (BDA). In this section we will develop basic tactics to aid you in conducting an airstrike by analyzing each of the above parts. Each individual situation will require modification of these basic tactics, but as fundamentals they will hold true. The effectiveness of the airborne forward air controller depends not only upon flying proficiency and knowledge, but also on the specific FAC's ability to adjust his tactics to meet changing orders-of-battle.

b. Mission Preparation - Mission preparation starts with the FAC's background knowledge of the operations area, of the operations of the friendly ground forces in it,and of the nature of his enemy. The FAC's job in visual reconnaissance makes him an intelligence gathering agent. This, coupled with the information from the Army Intelligence Section, and their sources, is the basis for target and area study. Once airborne, the FAC should complete any last minute surveillance without giving away his intentions of striking the particular target. Utilize the element of surprise! Plan your strike in your own mind. Normally, you will know the type of fighters and their ordnance load. You can plan the direction of the attack and break, matching this to the terrain and battle situation. Note the weather in the target area, particularly the wind. Plan your attack so that the smoke from the ordnance will not obscure the remainder of the target. Note the friendly towns and outposts and plan best bail-out areas for use should your fighters have difficulty; you are the expert on your area – your fighter pilots will look to you for this information. Also consider anticipated enemy ground fire for both your observation position and for your recommended fighter pattern. Even more basic is planning ahead to have complete charts and current operation overlays, current SOIs, aerial photographs (if available), and your personal survival equipment. A good aircraft pre-flight and FAC supervision of rocket loading, night-flare mounting, and smoke grenade loading might preclude embarrassing moments such as not pulling pins or having all violet smoke grenades aboard. (Violet smoke is the most difficult smoke color to be seen from the air.) Plan to be airborne at least 30 minutes prior to your scheduled fighter arrival time. Make a radio call to the Direct Air Request Net to let them know that you are airborne; advise them of your desired rendezvous location and working frequency. Next, coordinate your pending strike with the other friendly activities in the area. Now, finalize your fuel management plans – note your bingo time (that time at which you must depart the target in order to get to your airfield with a reasonable fuel reserve.)

c. The Rendezvous

(1) The rendezvous portion of the airstrike is the simple art of the FAC and fighters meeting at a predetermined area on a predetermined radio frequency. Time permitting, DASC and your ALO will coordinate the scheduled inbound fighter times, desired rendezvous location, and a working frequency prior to your takeoff; DASC will then advise the CRC of this information. Therefore, when you first check in on the Direct Air Request Net frequency, the CRC will be expecting you. Coordinate any last minute changes with them. Then, when your fighters check in on frequency you will be ready to proceed.

(2) Towns and significant landmarks are obvious rendezvous points. The name and UMT coordinates of the rendezvous will be passed to the fighters. These can be supplemented by TACAN positions. Be aware of the TACAN position of each prominent landmark in your area. Plan your rendezvous in the following manner: ". . . at the intersection of three large canals; TACAN position, Channel 41/020 degrees/17 nautical miles." Such a position will bring your fighters to your area, where you can make visual rendezvous. The classical method of completing rendezvous is for the FAC to meet the fighters at the predetermined location, then proceeding to the target. However, more than likely, your target will not be near a convenient rendezvous location. Now, if your target is ten miles from the rendezvous, it will probably take you ten minutes or more to fly this distance to the target. If your scheduled fighters are jets, they may only have 30 minutes total loiter and on-target time. Therefore, it will behoove you to hold near your target and to verbally direct your fighters to you from the scheduled rendezvous. Caution: insure that

your fighters are over the correct rendezvous location before you start giving them headings to fly. Once you have them in visual contact, you must direct their eyes to find you. The best method to use is the "clock" method; i.e. "I'm in your 2 o'clock position, low . . ." This sounds simple, but, add a little cloud cover, say 2000 feet scattered, and the problem becomes more complicated. Most Navy fighters and some USAF fighters will have a UHF homer. As you transmit to the fighters on UHF, they can "home-in" on you. This will make completing a rendezvous much easier. Once your fighters have arrived at their rendezvous and are flying to your exact location is the time to move into the next phase of the airborne FAC control of airstrikes, target description and markings.

d. Target Description and Marking

(1) Now, as you have established radio contact with your fighters and are making the rendezvous, this is the time to get information from your fighters and to brief them on your target.

(a) First, find out from the fighters number and type of aircraft, frag order mission number, ordnance load, time they can loiter and specific bingo time, altitude, and present location.

(b) Now, give the fighters a brief location of the target and nature of the target, height of terrain in target area, weather and surface winds, nearest friendly positions, best bailout position or heading, anticipated ground fire, restrictions on attack headings and breakaway directions, and where the FAC aircraft will hold.

(c) At this point, give a thorough briefing on your target if you have not already done so. Ask the flight leader in what order he wishes to drop his ordnance and plan last minute details of the attack.

(d) Complete visual rendezvous and enter target area.

(2) The actual marking of the target is, to some degree, a misnomer. The FAC may provide adequate target identification by verbal description. A smoke rocket or a smoke grenade may be used as common point of reference on the ground; however, often a good landmark is available from which the target can be described. In this case, a mark is not necessary. The mark gives away the specific intended target and the element of surprise is lost. Normally, one to four minutes elapse between target marking and a fighter pass. The enemy uses this time to disperse and take advantage of passive defenses. Realize, however, there is no substitute for an accurate mark. Utilize the element of surprise. Strive to describe and mark the target so that the first ordnance falls just after the "mark."

(3) A basic rule to remember is that the FAC IS THE EYES OF THE STRIKE PILOT. In describing target areas, be sure to talk in terms of landmarks easily visible and distinguishable from their higher altitude and faster airspeeds. First, advise the fighters of the nature of their target; i.e. "200 V.C. dug in along a canal, one heavy weapons platoon, anticipate moderate ground fire." Then start directing the eyes of the fighter pilots by starting at a known position on the ground or perhaps directly under your aircraft, and move their eyes by means of progressively smaller landmarks until you locate and describe the limits of the target; i.e. "Do you have the small village on my two o'clock position at two miles." "Roger." "Okay, that village is on a small east-west trail. Now, follow the trail to the west to the second bend toward the south. This is the southern limit of your target. Now, move your eyes northeast to a cleared area at 500 meters. Your target lies along a line between these points and 300 meters either side of it. On your low altitude passes you might be able to see a small trail hidden by the jungle."

e. Rocket Marking Procedures. On many FAC aircraft in SEA, there is no sight or permanent device on which to line up on a firing pass. The simplest method to make a sight is to place a grease pencil mark on the windshield to use as a sight. Fly the aircraft to an attitude where the rocket pods are level with the horizon and, looking straight ahead, place a mark on the windshield where the horizon crosses the center post. Be sure to remain in a normal sitting position while you are arriving at this point because your sitting height eye level and your windshield mark determine the sighting line. Keep the aircraft in coordinated flight while firing a rocket; i.e. keep the ball in the center of the case. There are many methods of establishing a rocket pass. Your instructor will demonstrate these so no attempts will be made to cover them here. However, a few basic rules are general.

(1) Analysis has proven that 1500 feet above the ground is a relatively safe altitude for protection from small arms ground fire. Therefore, plan to pull out from your pass by a minimum altitude of 1500 feet.

(2) The purpose of using a smoke marking rocket is to keep distance between you and the target. Do not yield this advantage.

(3) Confirm that the fighters have you in sight and advise them

that you will be marking in X seconds (15 to 30 seconds, normally).

(4) Do not get target fixation. Your job is to mark the target, not destroy it.

(5) For rocket marking, use about a 35 degree dive angle for optimum line-up on the target. Your next considerations will be to observe where your smoke mark hit and to put distance between you and the enemy. As you pull out from a rocket pass, plan to turn at least 90 degrees from your firing pass heading and perhaps all the way to 180 degrees; in the turn, roll up so that you can see the smoke hit. You can then begin to direct your fighters relative to it, while you are turning away from the target.

f. Smoke Grenades.

(1) To drop smoke grenades, fly a track directly across the target and drop the grenade just prior to reaching the target. If you make a low-level smoke drop, remember the safest level is on-the-treetops. Descend and climb out over known safe points. In any case, descend away from the target, fly over the target and, after dropping the smoke grenade, fly level away from the target before climbing; do not climb out immediately after dropping the marking smoke.

(2) After you have dropped the smoke grenade, then continue to fly basically straight ahead to give you the needed distance between you and the target. Bank the aircraft over and look for your smoke hit and begin to direct fighters. In either case, this mark serves only as reference point to insure that you and the fighters are talking about the same point. Be sure that the lead identifies the color of the smoke to lessen the effect of enemy deception or friendly confusion.

13. On-Target Control and Observation Positioning.

a. The task of the FAC is to position himself so as to adhere to two basic rules: (1) always be in position to see the fighters, and (2) always be in position to see the target. You must always be in position to see the fighters so that you can accomplish your share of midair collision avoidance and so that you can insure that the fighter is lined up on the proper target. You must be in position to see the target to make specific ordnance adjustments and so that you can observe the target for enemy activity and ground fire. These are two simple rules; however, you will find that to maintain such a position is not easy.

b. There are two basic patterns used to meet the above rules;

outside holding and overhead holding. Outside holding is the most basic pattern of the two. If your fighters have low altitude release ordnance, then the overhead holding pattern will suffice.

c. Should they have high angle, high release ordnance then an outside holding pattern will be best. Your best holding will be parallel to the fighter's inbound course on either side of the inbound but short of the release point line. This will keep you out of the pull-off area and will give the fighter more flexibility for evasive tactics on the pull-off without having to be primarily concerned over the location of the FAC.

d. The second basic pattern for use in controlling airstrikes is the overhead holding pattern. Take up a position directly over the target at an altitude of between 2000 and 3000 feet, and have your fighters work under you. This is a dangerous technique if moderate or heavy automatic weapons fire is encountered. However, if the FAC has done his homework with his respective intelligence officer, he will be aware of potential enemy action in the target area. This pattern will allow the fighters to better vary their attack headings and still be able to locate the FAC quickly on final approach.

e. There are many variations to the two basic patterns described above. On the outside pattern, rather than a racetrack pattern, fly an expanded figure eight with all turns toward the target. Using this figure eight you will find that by using your side and top visibility there is hardly any point in the pattern from which you cannot see both the fighters and the target.

f. Often it is imperative that you maintain a position close to the target in order to give the maximum assistance to your troops. If possible, make your holding position over the friendlies to reduce your exposure to the enemy. Remember to monitor your own fuel; in the heat of battle, time appears motionless. You will want to position yourself so that the smoke from the fires in the target will not obscure the target; on the other hand, if the ground fire is heavy, you may want to hide behind the smoke. Be sure to plan the fighter ordnance so that smoke from the first bomb will not obscure the remainder of the target.

g. Do not clear the fighter on a pass unless you have him in sight. A mid-air collision between you and a fighter or his ordnance could ruin your day. As each fighter nears his roll-in position, there are three bits of information that you will need:

(1) who he is, (2) where he is coming from, (3) what ordnance he is going to put on target; i.e. "Number three inbound from the west,

napalm." In this manner, you will be able to find the fighter quickly and provide a specific target for his ordnance. Have the strike aircraft make his inbound call prior to roll-in and, if you do not have him in sight, then have him abort the pass.

h. On restricting the final approach attack headings and breakaway directions, consider the following possibilities:

(1) The best direction of attack is generally parallel to friendly lines. You must also take into consideration long or short drops, runaway guns, obstacles, and known enemy ground fire.

(2) Often the breakaway direction will have to be restricted. You might have another airstrike in progress nearby that you must avoid. Also, you might have artillery firing at another objective; you must have the fighters avoid the "gunline." When you are striking within a valley bounded by high mountains, it is obvious that you must restrict the final approach heading.

(3) Even without the above limitations on the attack heading, it is recommended that you restrict the first aircraft on the target to the final approach heading on which you think that he will best be able to see the target. By doing this, you will gain the following information:

(a) The fighter pilots will get the best view of the target.

(b) You can establish the "timing" of the flight.

(c) You will be able to observe how accurate the flight is.

(d) You can get the "feel" of working with this flight under controlled conditions and observe their "combat savvy."

i. Following the initial pass by the flight leader, the FAC must direct subsequent attacks by the other members of the flight to insure adequate target destruction. One of the best methods is to provide adjustments in reference to the last ordnance on the target. Corrections should be given in meters from the last hit in relation to a distinguishable landmark, with the directions in cardinal compass headings. Using the terms "long, short, right, and left," can meet some situations; however, using cardinal compass headings, "north, south, east and west," will reduce the possibility of confusion when the fighters vary attack headings. You can use easily distinguishable landmarks to your best advantages: canals, houses, trails, tree lines, tree groups, contrasting tones of color, and even cloud shadows. Start your description from a readily identifiable object and move the fighter pilot's eyes from there to the desired impact area. For example, "From the last hit go southwest across the light green rice paddy, look for a house with a tin roof." While attempting to use standard phraseology, use any combination of the above methods if it is necessary to identify a specific target. With these tools, the FAC must give the strike pilots adjustments prior to the time that the fighter pilot rolls in on final approach. The information must be given quickly and curtly so the inbound pilot will have time for a question if he does not immediately pick out the target. The FAC must pick out a specific target for each pass, properly matching the target to the ordnance when possible. In other words, the FAC must plan the efficient distribution of ordnance. On-target control and observation positioning is like a puzzle, only you must determine which parts are necessary and which parts can be used. The final solution to each situation may be different; thus, we find problem-solving at its best.

j. Once again we reiterate that 1500 feet should be your minimum altitude for your reconnaissance work and airstrikes not involving anti-aircraft weapons. Any exception to this must be evaluated to meet a specific situation. Normally, when comparing the risk against the results to be gained, there is little to be gained by flying lower. As much as possible, close surveillance should be accomplished prior to the airstrike. Flying at a lower altitude will only increase exposure to battle damage. On using 1500 feet as a standard altitude, keep in mind that small arms is effective to 1500 feet and that 50 cal. is effective to about 6500 feet (max about 23000); add to this consideration the sophistication of the weapon – choose your flying altitude accordingly.

13.1 Bomb Damage Assessment (BDA). The last strike responsibility of the FAC is the bomb damage assessment. The BDA is simply what it implies, a word picture of the damage inflicted on the target. "Five houses destroyed; seven houses damaged; two large sampans sunk; one large secondary explosion from a sampan due to strafe; encountered automatic weapons fire, position destroyed - bombs; 40 percent target coverage. Remarks, excellent bombing accuracy." The classical method for the FAC to obtain this BDA is to re-enter the target area following the strike and examine the damage. This is dangerous and, unless the FAC has orders to get special information, it is not worth the added battle exposure. If the FAC has done his work correctly, he will have completed the BDA simultaneously with the strike. Specific information that you should give the fighters is as follows: target coordinates, percent target destroyed, itemized destruction, time on and off target and remarks.

14. Close Air Support. Close air support is the ultimate mission of the FAC. Working in close coordination with ground forces is perhaps the most rewarding mission in which the FAC can participate. No matter how well planned a ground operation has been, when solid contact with the enemy is made, the situation changes, even becoming desperate. As a FAC, your observation and interpretations when passed to the field command post of the ground forces become of tremendous value to the commander in making maneuvering decisions. Thus, your job is instrumental to the immediate battle situation. In those operations your airstrikes will be highly restricted as opposed to more simple interdiction targets. Your preplanned airstrikes in the operations area will clear the way for helilifts and armor plunges. Following these strikes, you will move into an observation phase, aiding the ground navigation. Keeping note of the exact location of your maneuvering forces is most important because if desperate contact is made and airstrikes are needed, this will greatly affect the conduct of your strike. The ground commander may decide to continue firing artillery during your airstrike on an adjacent target; in this case you will have to be aware of the gun target line and restrict the fighters from that area. Also, you will have to be aware of the working area of helicopter gunships in the area. And last, there may be another airstrike taking place nearby. When you add to the situation, confused and irregular friendly battle lines, and compound it by poor communications, then you will have an idea of the problem to be solved. There is not intended to be one solution to these situations; herein is the value of an airborne FAC.

a. Usually when situations like these arise, and excellent communications are needed, then Murphy's Law applies and communications get worse. It seems that everyone that has a radio comes up on frequency and wants an immediate situation report. Add to this normal battle chatter and you will be quite busy monitoring two or three radios. You will have to tolerate this until such time that your fighters check in on frequency. At this time you will have to assume role number one (during an airstrike, the FAC is in command), and, if necessary, demand that all stations minimize chatter. Set your radios up in the following manner. Monitor FM for ground-to-air frequency; brief your ground commander that as each ordnance hits the ground for him to give you his desired adjustment; also brief him that you may or may not acknowledge his transmission and that the fighter ordnance may not follow his exact instructions because from your perch you can see the overall situation. Now use UHF for air-to-air control of your fighters. Thus, it will only be necessary for you to use one frequency to transmit on. This set-up has been proven quite successful.

b. One problem that may arise is several flights of fighters arriving at rendezvous at or about the same time. It is quite difficult to control these inbound fighters while also working a flight in close air support. It will greatly assist you to have the ground ALO in the field command post or another airborne FAC to control the holding stack, giving a general briefing to them, and feeding the flights to you as you need them. This can save much time and this time can be most important if the flights do not have much loiter time.

15. Night Airstrikes.

a. Although a very small percentage of your work will occur at night, a few generalities here may aid you. Darkness can be as great an aid to you as it can be to the enemy. First, fly blacked-out; do not give the enemy a target. The vast majority of your airstrikes at night will be with the aid of a flare ship. This flare ship will fly approximately 3500 feet, keeping your target lighted. Do not attempt to direct the flare ship, just show him the area that you want lighted; he will determine the frequency of flare drops. Should you be working on a moonlight night, you will have few problems. A dark night can present many problems.

b. If you know that you are going to have a night strike, then plan to carry parachute night flares on two of your wing stations. After you have found the target and your flare ship has arrived, you can save a long briefing by dropping one of your flares on the target area to show what you would like to keep lighted. Whole controlling a flight of fighters under a flare ship, avoid flying in the lighted area as you will be illuminated directly and will be the only target visible for the enemy on the ground. The principle of controlling airstrikes will remain the same. You will be able to determine the enemy positions rapidly as you will be able to see tracer fire and muzzle flashes. On the ground, the night belongs to the enemy. Be aware of your lessened chances of rescue at night. Do not over-extend yourself.

SECTION E – VISUAL RECONNAISSANCE

21. Recommendations for Conducting Visual Reconnaissance:

a. Work closely with the intelligence and operations sections of the ground unit to which attached. Prior to every flight, the FACs should know all reported and suspected locations of enemy activity and the exact boundaries of all specified strike zones; in addition, the

FAC needs to have detailed information on all friendly units, including present position, planned movement, call signs, and frequencies.

b. At all times while airborne, carefully examine the area below for signs of enemy activity, regardless of the type of mission being flown. When practicable, plan all flights to maximize VR coverage, for example; select a route proceeding to and from an airstrike target to overfly probable areas of enemy activity nearby.

c. Establish a system to insure that all portions of your area receive periodic VR coverage, giving frequent attention to the more likely enemy locations; however, avoid following a set timetable which would allow the enemy to plan their activities around your coverage.

d. On all flights, carry 1:50,000 scale maps of your area of responsibility. Carry similar maps of adjacent areas. You might need them in an emergency. Always keep track of your position on the appropriate maps, and immediately plot and annotate any significant sighting directly on your map.

e. Study the appearance of the terrain and the general behavior patterns of the people throughout your area. Know what to expect to see, and be suspicious of any deviation from the normal – the presence of these could well be the cause of the disruption.

(1) Learn the eating, sleeping, working, traveling, and social routines of the people.

(2) Know the normal harvesting processing, distribution, and storage procedures for all crops grown in your area.

(3) Check villages and fields for the normal percentage of men, as compared to women and children.

(4) Check dirt roads and trails for amount of usage, keeping in mind the reason for their existence. Remember that rain will wash away old wheel marks and the resulting mud will record travel since the rain; remember that the enemy operates primarily at night, so checking a trail at sunset and then again at the following sunrise could detect usage by the enemy.

(5) Check roads for cuts and any sign of digging which could indicate mining; also, check along roads and waterways for possible ambush sites, indicated by trenches and foxholes.

(6) Check shorelines and banks along waterways for marks in the mud and disturbed foliage which could indicate enemy activity. At dawn and when the tide is out are good times to cover these areas.

(7) In the early morning and late afternoon, look for shadows in otherwise flat terrain – they could be caused by enemy bunkers. Shadows are also useful in determining the height of an object, by com-

parison with the shadow produced by something of known height.

(8) Remember that the enemy goes to great lengths to avoid detection from the air – his facilities are small and well camouflaged, and often completely underground in the form of caves and tunnels. In addition, people are very difficult to spot from the air unless they are in the open; consequently, stay alert for indications of human activity (i.e. smoke from campfires and disturbed flocks of birds) in suspect areas.

f. Before making a general VR of your area, check specific points of interest obtained from the Army Intelligence and Operations Sections. Start scanning the area of the point of interest from as far out as possible – as soon as the enemy realizes an aircraft is approaching, they will take steps to avoid discovery by dousing cooking fires, etc.; a wisp of smoke may be the only indication you can find, so plot it immediately, before it disappears.

g. When checking a specific point, start from the coordinates provided by the Army Intelligence Section. If you find nothing, imagine yourself as the enemy commander and check out any other likely points nearby.

h. At all times, avoid flying a straight line or a predictable flight path, such as staying directly above the river; frequently random turns makes your aircraft a more difficult target for ground fire. Also, analysis has proven that an altitude of 1500 feet above the ground is relatively safe for light aircraft subject to small arms ground fire.

i. To detect specific objects on the ground, stare at a point for a few seconds, then shift your stare to another point, continuing until you have covered the desired area by focusing on a succession of points. General area scanning (as used to spot other aircraft) is ineffective due to the lack of contrast between possible enemy targets and the surrounding terrain.

j. Check the area to the rear of the aircraft, as well as to the front and either side; personnel may feel safe to move about after the aircraft has passed.

k. If you spot a possible target, avoid a flight path which would indicate to the enemy that they have been discovered. If possible, continue your flight path as before the sighting and depart the area; draw a detailed mental picture of the target in your mind -when the target is no longer visible, make notes and sketches as needed. Always try to avoid making an immediate turn to overfly the target, and do not make repeated passes in the target vicinity. If the enemy is not alerted, the impending airstrike will be much more effective.

1. In some areas, heavy tree cover may completely obscure any view of the ground when flying at 1500 feet above the terrain. If mission accomplishment is keyed to check an area of this type, you may elect to conduct VR at a lower altitude. If you decide to go below 1500 feet in heavily tree-covered areas, a few feet above the tree tips is the next safest altitude for protection from small arms ground fire. Descend and climb out over known safe points.

m. The FAC should know the indicators that signify the enemy's presence or activity. Some of the indicators are as follows:

(1) Tracks: human, animal and vehicle, indicating increased or recent travel. Water-soaked earth near a puddle or stream and tracks around new bomb craters indicate recent passage. Often direction of travel can be determined by noting the position of the damp ground in relation to the water.

(2) Movement of supplies or farming in an isolated area – farming may be indicated by drying grain or clothes, harvesting, or increased cattle population.

(3) Newly turned earth indicates foxholes, caves, tunneling.

(4) Camouflage is evidence of something being hidden. Well camouflaged items may be hard to detect.

(5) The use of shadows is a key method of noting camouflage. At noon there are few shadows; optimum shadows occur early in the morning and late in the afternoon.

(6) Gun positions – occupants may be hidden in the positions or nearby under foliage or in foxholes. If you find obvious positions, closely VR the surrounding area to insure that they are not "sucker" positions causing you to miss nearby actual positions.

(7) Sampans – unusual numbers, position or activity.

(8) People running and trying to hide or the complete lack of activity in an obviously occupied area.

n. What the enemy does when he thinks he has been spotted varies constantly and may be affected by terrain, training, situation, etc. The following are reactions to the presence of FACs in the past and some guidance on where to look for the enemy.

(1) Usually the enemy will stop and try to hide by blending into the background, especially near bunkers or camouflaged items. He may hide under cattle or try to imitate a bush, tree or dike.

(2) If he thinks he is exposed, he will scurry for cover like a rat, running in short bursts from cover to cover. He moves when your aircraft is pointed away and freezes when you fly toward him. This necessitates watching to the rear as well as forward to spot enemy activity.

(3) The enemy may change dress and hide his weapons to blend with the local population, or take off his hat and clothes, arrange them on the ground and escape the area while the FAC circles the decoy clothing.

(4) Enemy base camps are often found near well-used trails and trail intersections, near cultivated areas along ridge lines or off of the main ridge line and near cleared areas under trees.

o. Ground fire is usually heard rather than seen. If the source of ground fire is seen, the muzzle flash looks like a yellow strobe with a puff of smoke during the day and white strobe at night. Tracers leave a red streak but are usually used only by regular troops under attack. Snipers seldom use tracers unless they aren't worried about disclosing their position.

p. Light aircraft are not designed or equipped to combat ground fire; therefore, areas of known or suspected enemy ground fire should be avoided whenever possible, especially at low altitude. The FAC should always vary his maneuvers and patterns and never repeat in an area of suspected or known ground fire. In areas of jungle cover, the trees tend to give some protection, unless the FAC flies directly over the enemy or across an open area. Often dropping a smoke grenade may cause the enemy to cease fire in an effort to escape the airstrike which usually follows a FAC's mark.

q. The FAC must be alert at all times for other aircraft, realizing he is hard to see and has little chance for survival should a mid-air collision occur. It is also the FAC's responsibility to keep the fighters informed of other known aircraft in the area.

r. You may feel that your VR has produced a target worthy of an airstrike immediately. If so, try to get it approved and get strike aircraft. In any case, report all sightings to the Army Intelligence Section as soon as possible after each flight.

s. Target approval authority varies in different areas and specific assignments. This approval authority is closely associated with the "Rules of Engagement."